THRIVE
ON PRESSURE

THRIVE ON PRESSURE

■■■

LEAD AND SUCCEED WHEN TIMES GET TOUGH

■■■

GRAHAM JONES, PH.D.

New York   Chicago   San Francisco   Lisbon   London   Madrid   Mexico City
Milan   New Delhi   San Juan   Seoul   Singapore   Sydney   Toronto

Copyright © 2010 by The McGraw-Hill Companies, Inc. All rights reserved. Printed in the United States of America. Except as permitted under the United States Copyright Act of 1976, no part of this publication may be reproduced or distributed in any form or by any means, or stored in a database or retrieval system, without the prior written permission of the publisher.

1 2 3 4 5 6 7 8 9 10 11 12 13 14 15 16   WFR/WFR   1 9 8 7 6 5 4 3 2 1 0

ISBN 978-0-07-174882-7
MHID   0-07-174882-2

This publication is designed to provide accurate and authoritative information in regard to the subject matter covered. It is sold with the understanding that neither the author nor the publisher is engaged in rendering legal, accounting, securities trading, or other professional services. If legal advice or other expert assistance is required, the services of a competent professional person should be sought.
    —*From a Declaration of Principles Jointly Adopted by a Committee of the American Bar Association and a Committee of Publishers and Associations*

Library of Congress Cataloging-in-Publication Data

Jones, J. Graham.
        Thrive on pressure : lead and succeed when times get tough / by Graham Jones.
            p.   cm.
        Includes index.
        ISBN 978-0-07-174882-7 (alk. paper)
        1. Leadership.   2. Stress (Psychology)   3. Crisis management.   I. Title.

HD57.7.J657 2011
658.4'092—dc22   2010025514

McGraw-Hill books are available at special quantity discounts to use as premiums and sales promotions or for use in corporate training programs. To contact a representative, please e-mail us at bulksales@mcgraw-hill.com.

This book is printed on acid-free paper.

To Mum and Dad

Contents

■ ■ ■

Acknowledgments

■ ■ ■

I love what I do for a living, and I feel privileged to have had some amazing experiences and opportunities. I owe this to the elite athletes and leaders who have allowed me into their lives. I have grown enormously from my interactions with them, and I hope they have too.

Thank you to Professor Sheldon Hanton and Dr. Declan Connaughton. The foundations of this book are based on the research we carried out together.

Thank you to Dr. Tara Jones for her unwavering belief in me as well as her feedback on the content.

Thank you to Theresa Ludwick for her unrelenting support in making this happen.

Thank you to David Wilk for his advice and guidance through the publishing process.

Thank you to Tiana Kennedy for helping me with my "technophobe" challenges in putting the more complex bits of the manuscript together.

Finally, thank you to Tara, Emma, Kellee, Ben, Andy, Jack, Libby, Charlie, and Calum. They all know how important they are in my life, but I wanted to remind them here.

Introduction

■ ■ ■

Are You Willing to Put Yourself on the Line?

This is not another book on *how* to lead; there are tons of those books out there already! Instead, this is a book on how to *deal* with the pressure that is an inevitable and inescapable part of being a leader, and how you can use it to your advantage. But first you must make a choice about how much you are willing to put on the line as a leader.

I emerged into the business arena from a world where leadership, pressure, and performance are inseparable. As a sports psychologist working at the highest levels, I consulted with athletes who had chosen to put themselves on the line. Their highly visible and measurable performances meant they had to commit anything and everything on the world's largest stages—the Olympic Games and world championships—if they wanted to become number one. However, I spent as much time with their coaches as I did with the athletes! Coaches are the business leader equivalents who are hired and fired based on the results their performers deliver. They are the leaders who put everything on the line, but whose success or failure is largely out of their hands once their athletes have crossed over the white lines and onto the playing field. Sometimes, they watch helplessly as their best-laid plans disintegrate in front of them in a display of ineptitude and mediocrity. But they know there is no hiding place; this is the stage they have chosen for themselves, and they know the buck stops with them.

It soon became apparent during my early forays into the business world that sports is a powerful metaphor for business leadership. The incessant pursuit of excellence, the ferocious competition that often culminates in winning and losing by the tiniest margin, formulating strategies and tactics for the long and short term, hard work, perseverance, guts and determination, teamwork, basking in the highs of success, and bouncing back from the lows of failure and setbacks are all fundamental elements of both worlds.

At the core of success in sports and business is the ability to continually raise performance to higher levels. The central focus is on goals and standards that move onward and upward, resulting in a never-ending search for new ways of achieving targets that at times seem out of reach. It is not surprising that one of the biggest determinants of success is the ability to perform to consistently high levels under pressure—that accepted and expected part of top-level sports that makes it such a great spectacle. But it is not quite the same in the business world where such intense, unrelenting, and often unwanted pressure can make or break leaders.

This book is aimed at what I call *real* leaders—those of you who have the guts to put yourselves out there and make a real difference to the organization you work for, as well as the teams and people you lead. Most important, it will help you to deal better with the pressure you encounter, and even thrive in the most difficult times.

Leadership and Mental Toughness

A considerable amount of my work in the business world has involved supporting leaders in roles that are increasingly engulfed in pressure amidst tough times. In some cases, I have helped them cope with overwhelming circumstances that threatened the existence of their organizations. But merely *coping* with pressure is insufficient to be a *real* leader. *Real* leaders do more than cope with pressure—they *thrive* on it! And the vital factor that enables them to thrive on pressure is the development and enhancement of mental toughness.

Over the last few years, I have been working with senior business leaders to develop a level of mental toughness that enables them to deliver consistently high levels of performance under pressure. I have no doubt that you are reading this book because you, too, would like to deliver consistently high levels of performance under pressure. You may have already reached a high level in the corporate world and want to continue your development to achieve even greater things. Alternatively, you may have high potential and be looking for ways to aspire to your own and others' high expectations of you as a future leader.

Book Overview

This book is intended to be thought provoking, to raise awareness, and, most important, to provide you with tools and strategies that will develop and enhance your mental toughness so you can excel at being a *real* leader. Every effort has been made to ensure the topics of *real* leadership and mental toughness are easily understandable and actionable via simple frameworks that illustrate the key components of the various elements of *real* leadership and mental toughness. Stories about some of the leaders I have coached and worked with are also included in order to bring to life how the core principles of mental toughness apply to *real* leaders.

Content

The book is divided into five master classes. I use the words *master classes* because I assume that you already have the knowledge and experience of what it takes to be a leader and how to cope with the associated pressures. Also, you may already be pretty good at some of the skills and tools covered. The content of the book is therefore intended to build on your knowledge and experience. The master classes, together with the chapters that comprise each, are outlined briefly below.

Master Class 1: *Real* Leadership, Pressure, and Mental Toughness

Chapter 1 explores the many demands on leaders and, in particular, the visibility and exposure that often come with the role.

Chapter 2 identifies the different motives that underpin my distinction between *real* and *safe* leaders and how these drive leader behaviors.

Chapter 3 describes how *real* leaders create high-performance environments and concludes by introducing the key role of mental toughness in helping *real* leaders to thrive on pressure.

Chapter 4 takes a close look at pressure, before addressing what mental toughness is in *real* leaders. The chapter concludes by identifying the four key skills of mental toughness: staying in control under stress, strengthening your self-belief, channeling your motivation to work *for* you, and directing your focus to the things that *really* matter.

Master Class 2: Staying in Control Under the Inevitable Stress That Comes with Being a *Real* Leader

Chapter 5 looks at the two faces of pressure: a positive one that energizes you so that you thrive and a negative one that causes stress. It introduces three ways of dealing with the stress you experience as a *real* leader: controlling your symptoms, challenging the thinking that causes you stress, and tackling the sources of your stress.

Chapter 6 focuses on the symptoms you experience when you are stressed and describes different strategies and tools for controlling these symptoms.

Chapter 7 examines the different thought patterns that can lead to stress and how you can gain control over them.

Chapter 8 addresses the circumstances that are the source of your stress, concluding with an exercise that drives an action plan to deal with them.

Master Class 3: Strengthening Your Self-Belief in Your Ability as a *Real* Leader

Chapter 9 describes how it is easier to thrive on pressure when you believe in yourself. It explains how your level of self-belief in your ability as a *real* leader is a function of the relationship between your self-esteem and self-confidence. This chapter goes on to define these fundamental elements of self-belief.

Chapter 10 focuses on ways of enhancing your self-esteem in the context of how you respond to feedback and how you attribute success and failure. It also focuses on your achievements and how they can be used as important sources of self-esteem. This chapter concludes by describing how tackling any perfectionist tendencies will help improve your self-esteem.

Chapter 11 describes a variety of tools and strategies that can be used for boosting your self-confidence in specific situations.

Master Class 4: Channeling Your Motivation to Work *for* You in Your Role as a *Real* Leader

Chapter 12 reveals how it is not the *level* but rather the *nature* of your motivation that is critical in enabling you to thrive on the pressures of being a *real* leader. This chapter guides you through some key aspects of motivation and describes how you can ensure that your own motivation is "healthy" so that it works *for* rather than *against* you.

Chapter 13 describes the basic essentials of setting effective goals in order to optimize your motivation. It also introduces frameworks that provide you with a means of structuring and planning your goals to maximize their effectiveness.

Master Class 5: Directing Your Focus to the Things That *Really* Matter in Your Role as a *Real* Leader

Chapter 14 deals with the many potential distractions you encounter as a *real* leader and helps you identify what you *should* be focused on when under pressure.

Chapter 15 looks at the relationship between focus and mental toughness and describes specific strategies for controlling your focus so that you are able to attend to the things that *really* matter when you are under pressure.

Over to You: Your *Real* Leader Toolkit

Chapter 16 draws together the content of the master classes in the form of a toolkit of reminders about the choices you are committing to as a *real* leader, the core principles you should follow in creating a high-performance environment, and the tools you can use to develop and enhance your ability to thrive on pressure.

Getting the Most from the Book

As you work your way through the master classes, there are a number of Time-Out sections that ask you to take a few moments to reflect and build on your growing understanding of mental toughness and how you can develop and enhance it. To maximize your investment of time in reading the book, I strongly encourage you to complete each Time-Out as you come to it. It will be helpful to keep a notebook nearby to record your reflections and conclusions as you progress through the book.

I have designed the content and layout of the book with the intention that you can consult separate master classes for guidance on how to develop and enhance specific elements of *real* leadership and mental toughness. However, I do encourage you to read the book in its entirety, and then keep it close at hand as a constant reminder of the *real* leader you are striving hard to be and the mental toughness you will require along the way.

Master Class 1

■ ■ ■

Real Leadership, Pressure, and Mental Toughness

OBJECTIVES

■ To clarify the responsibilities and accountabilities of leaders, and the associated pressures

■ To distinguish between *real* and *safe* leaders

■ To establish the role and expectations of *real* leaders

■ To introduce mental toughness and to define what it is in *real* leaders

■ ■ ■

Chapter 1

■ ■ ■

No Hiding Place for Leaders

KEY TOPICS

■ The key responsibilities and accountabilities of leaders
■ The pressures on leaders
■ Leading in turbulent times

Leading Is Tough

If you believe what you read in the multitude of books on leadership, then you will know just how hard it is to be a good leader. The list below is by no means exhaustive of the qualities and skills that, according to these books, are required to be a good leader, but it serves to demonstrate the complex and diverse nature of a role that can at times seem overwhelming. Apparently, being a good leader requires you to:

- *Be a good communicator*
- *Have a clear vision*
- *Be a meticulous planner*
- *Make the right decisions*
- *Be self-assured*
- *Be a good people manager*
- *Instill belief*
- *Be inspiring*
- *See the big picture*

- *Be intellectually astute*
- *Show passion*
- *Be a mentor*
- *Have a high tolerance for stress and pressure*
- *Be a good listener*
- *Know the relevant detail*
- *Problem solve*
- *Remain calm in the face of adversity*
- *Be optimistic*
- *Know your people's names*
- *Have a high level of emotional intelligence*
- *Be a team player*
- *Learn from your mistakes*
- *Care about your people*
- *Be innovative*
- *Show empathy*
- *Be visible*
- *Let people make mistakes*
- *Balance the short and long term*
- *Address underperformance*
- *Command loyalty from your people*
- *Empower people*
- *Handle conflict*
- *Deliver the strategy*
- *Recognize good performance*
- *Delegate*
- *Recruit good people around you*
- *Be a good negotiator*
- *Ensure change*
- *Tell it like it is*
- *Be determined*
- *Have integrity*
- *Take risks*
- *Trust people*
- *Have charisma*

- *Be a good influencer*
- *Involve people in decisions*
- *Coach*
- *Be your own person*
- *Seek feedback*
- *Be able to give bad news*
- *Set goals*
- *Build team spirit*
- *Know what drives your people*
- *Make people accountable*
- *Role model the organization's values*
- *Set high expectations*
- *Deliver the results*

And, by the way, while you are working hard to focus on and do all these things well, don't forget to achieve a good work-life balance!

No Hiding Place for Leaders

I know from my experiences of working with senior executives that being a leader can be tough. Leaders are hired and fired based on their ability, or lack of it, to inspire their people to deliver the performance demanded by key stakeholders. There is no place for leaders to hide when the stakes are this high. At the most fundamental level, as shown in Figure 1.1, their job is to establish a clear vision for the organization, business unit, or team they lead; their people want to know *where* their leader intends to take them. Next, leaders need to formulate a strategy and plan so their people know *how* the vision will be achieved and what is expected of them. The vision, strategy, and plan must then be communicated to the people who are being asked to deliver it. This is the point where leaders must exhibit a level of logic that is bulletproof if they are to secure their people's buy-in and

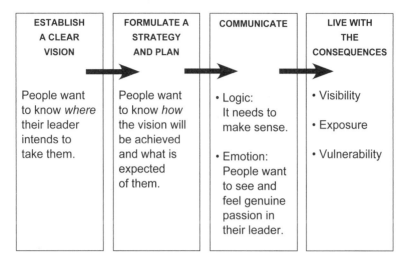

Figure 1.1 No Hiding Place for Leaders

engagement. In communicating the vision and strategy, leaders must also show genuine emotion, oozing a passion that will inspire everyone to follow. This whole process means they will be highly visible and vulnerable.

Many of the senior leaders I have worked with are so exposed that they sometimes feel isolated and lonely. Everyone wants to be their friend. In fact, they have so many "friends" that they are sometimes unable to identify who their true friends and allies are.

Such visibility can weigh very heavily on the shoulders of leaders. The expectations of their people and of themselves can be enormous, to the extent they may secretly wonder if they are up to it. Behind closed doors, I have been told by a number of senior executives, "Graham, I'm waiting to be found out" or "Graham, I'm wondering how I got to this position; I don't feel comfortable in it."

Take Ted, for example, who was the managing director of a retail company. The company had enjoyed year-on-year steady growth in a niche retail market for some time. Spotting the potential to grow into a wider market, a venture capitalist invested heavily in the company. For Ted, the managing director role now became a different proposition: he had to answer to new stakeholders who demanded substantial and rapid growth. He was responsible for establishing the new vision, formulating the strategy and plan, and then inspiring his people to deliver the goods. There was no hiding place for Ted. We talked at length about the huge expectations on him and how his exposure had led to a loneliness and vulnerability that unnerved him. He was having sleepless nights and wondered if he was up to it.

The accountabilities of leaders do not, of course, cease when they have secured the buy-in of people via a compelling vision delivered with passion. The demands are incessant as leaders become dominated by the daily grind of operating in an environment where they are expected to be decisive, know the answers, be role models, and deliver the results. Get it wrong, and you can lose many of those newly acquired "friends and allies."

My most vivid experience of working with someone who found himself in this position was in the field of sports. Rick coached a team that regularly attracted numerous inches of column space in the newspapers. He was highly visible and had gained respect from expectant fans when the early part of his tenure brought the success they had longed for. His team was successful and he was a hero. But things began to derail when his team lost to lesser opposition in two back-to-back poor performances. Before long, his team was in the middle of its worst run since he took charge, and it got worse. Media that had built Rick up to be a great coach quickly became his biggest critic. He stopped reading the newspapers and watching television sports news. He stopped going out in public because the open abuse he received from fans who spotted him was intolerable. When the team enjoyed success, Rick had been surrounded by people who wanted to share in it. Now the failure was his alone to bear. This new place he found himself in was a very lonely one; he was exposed and highly vulnerable.

Rick continued to prepare the team before each game in the best way he knew. He continued to deliver rousing team talks before each game and then watched from the sideline as tens of thousands of expectant fans and media hungry for a sensational headline judged whether or not he had done a good job. He was accountable for his team's performance but was virtually helpless once the contest began. I ventured into this pressure-cooker environment anticipating that I would be working closely with the team. Instead, I spent the majority of my time supporting Rick. After one particularly painful defeat he asked me if he should resign. Rick had lost sight of how to deal with the pressure. He had become too focused on the things that were going wrong and had lost belief in himself and his undoubted ability as a coach. This is what pressure can do to leaders when things go wrong.

Leadership Is About People, and People Are Hard to Lead

People get promoted to leadership positions because they are good at what they do. But leadership is not about being a good accountant, engineer, lawyer, mathematician, investment banker, and the like. The mistake most organizations make is to move people up through the organization because of what they have achieved using their functional skills, experience, and expertise. They then find themselves having to bring someone like myself in to help these leaders understand how to lead their people.

Leadership is about people, and people are hard to lead! They have opinions and views on how things should be done. Some of them may think they can do a better job at leading than you. They have feelings, moods, and emotions that are sometimes unpredictable, unexpected, and inexplicable. Their motivation, confidence, and personalities all need to be factored into any interactions. They have frailties and make mistakes. They like to be praised and made to feel good about themselves. Some of them want responsibility, while others want to be told what to do. Some of them are to be trusted; others are not. Some are loyal to their leader; others are not.

All these ways in which people differ, and the many more too numerous to list, mean that leading is hard. This is why many leaders focus on managing tasks and operations—it is a lot easier than leading people!

And That Does Not Include the Turbulent Times!

If all of the above does not constitute a demanding enough challenge, then leaders are certainly tested when times are tough. Good economic climates hide many flaws in corporations, and poor or inept leadership often goes unnoticed in those favorable times. Too often, as long as the results are delivered, few questions are asked about "*how*" they are delivered. But things are very different when times are tough. Leaders have never been more visible than during the recent dramatic difficulties facing the business world. These roller-coaster times have engulfed large corporations that seemed untouchable. This is when outstanding leadership is so crucial; of course, it also just happens to be when outstanding leadership is so very difficult to deliver! Because employees need and want to be able to trust their leaders in these difficult times, being open and letting them know how things stand is paramount. Recognizing that an inevitable part of change and turbulent times is that there will be a fair amount of catastrophizing and doom-and-gloom among their people is also required because leaders will need to help them deal with it. Listening to their concerns, showing empathy, and reminding them of the successes, however small (there will be some, even though they might have to look hard for them), always has to be at the forefront of the leader's mind in these circumstances. But leaders must also continue to focus on a strategy for moving forward and keeping their people focused on delivering quality service and products to their customers.

Building Organizational Resilience

This is where having a vision for getting through the tough times is so important. Leaders often misconstrue visions as a grand statement or series of statements that reference only how an organization or business unit will conquer their industry sector in the next five or maybe ten years. Visions like these get lost easily in tough times, when survival over the next six months might be the core ambition and focus. Leaders can too often become embroiled, instead, in day-to-day firefighting and short-termism, trusting that hard work and long hours will see them through. What many leaders fail to understand is that visions are just as—if not more—important during turbulent times. But they are not visions about conquering the world, and they may be in the form of short-term aspirations. These are visions of how the organization, business unit, or team will deal with the current difficulties and emerge stronger. This type of vision is about organizational resilience,[1] reminding people what they are good at, what is required from them, and telling a story of how the challenges will be overcome.

1. K. Walsh, "From fragile to agile: Developing a framework of organizational resilience," *The Lane4 Journal of Excellence*, November 2008, 30–40.

The best example of this in my experience of working with leaders in tough times is Sam, the head of a building materials organization experiencing a serious downturn in a rapidly shrinking economy. In the midst of announcing job losses, Sam also spent time telling the people left behind his vision of how the organization would emerge from its difficulties stronger than when it entered them. He reminded his people of their skills and abilities, and the resilience they had showed in previous downturns. He talked about how people would grow and develop during the tough times ahead and how the organization would retain its top talent to ensure it maintained its competitive advantage when better times returned. Sam told them how they would find opportunities they could seize on because of the optimism they would carry forward over the next few months. Here was a great example of a short-term vision of the resilience required in tough times.

Being Stretched to the Limit

All this is demanded of leaders, of course, when they may be feeling pretty worried and pessimistic themselves! Clients, employees, shareholders, and the media are but a few of the stakeholders who watch leaders very carefully indeed to see how they cope under such circumstances.

So in turbulent economic markets, even the best leaders are stretched to their limits. What has worked in the past may not work in these difficult times. This is the time when the pressure cooker leaders find themselves in either makes or breaks them.

So Why Would Anyone Want to Be a Leader?

I have deliberately painted a dark side of leadership to emphasize just how demanding it is if you are to do it well. When you
do get it right, it is very enjoyable and satisfying; that's one of the
important reasons why people are attracted to leading. And the
good news is that there are many stories about leaders who have
really struggled in the role to begin with, or at various points in
their tenure, then turned things around and learned to thrive on
the pressure. For example, I am sure you will be glad to know
that Ted and Rick, the leaders I referred to earlier in this chapter
as having problems dealing with their exposure and vulnerability,
learned how to deal with their circumstances via a number of different strategies and tools described later in this book.

KEY TAKEAWAYS

- The role of leaders is complex and diverse.
- This complexity and diversity is exacerbated in
  turbulent times.
- When leaders perform their roles effectively, they
  are visible and exposed.
- Leading is enjoyable and satisfying when you get
  it right.

Chapter 2

■ ■ ■

Being a *Real* Leader

KEY TOPICS

■ The difference between *real* and *safe* leaders
■ Being a *real* leader in turbulent times
■ What type of leader are *you*?

The core theme of the previous chapter was that leading can be tough. This chapter describes and examines the differences between *real* leaders who are up for the challenge and *safe* leaders who quite literally go for a safer option.

Real and *Safe* Leaders

Have you ever considered why leaders choose to be leaders? Is it about the status, package, power, and authority that come with the role? Is it the responsibility, accountability, and vision required that attracts them? Or is it about the opportunity to make a difference and have a real impact? In fact, what has driven *you* to choose to be a leader?

My experience of coaching numerous senior leaders in Fortune 500 and FTSE 100 companies has led to my realization that they

have different motives for being leaders. Based on these obser-
vations and experiences, I have identified two types of leader
that I call *real* and *safe*.[2] This distinction has been apparent to
me across all market conditions, but it has been particularly evident in turbulent times. It is the tough economic conditions that
bring with them an intriguing quandary for leaders. These are
the times when leaders must make a choice between opting for
safe leadership or choosing to step up to be *real* leaders. Some
of the key differences between *safe* and *real* leaders that I have
encountered are shown in Table 2.1.

Safe Leaders	*Real* Leaders
• Are driven by their need for rewards, status, and power and are therefore unwilling to put themselves on the line because of the threat of losing their position if they get it wrong	• Are driven much more by the challenge and opportunity to put themselves out there and make a difference; this is what leadership is about for them
• Focus on tasks	• Focus on people
• Focus on "what to do" to ensure they conform to company practices and procedures	• Focus on "how to be" so they provide good role models for their people
• Say they are too busy to focus on the future	• Make time to focus on the future
• Rarely innovate or challenge ortho-doxy during their tenure because their focus is almost exclusively on micro-managing the short term	• Empower others to focus on manag-ing short-term challenges so their own minds can be more focused on innovating and investing in the future
• React mainly to immediate day-to-day ongoing issues	• Create a road map for the future
• Are reluctant to be under the spotlight	• Accept that they are highly visible
• Are reluctant to receive feedback that highlights areas for improvement	• Are hungry for feedback that helps them develop
	continued on next page

Table 2.1 Key Differences Between *Safe* and *Real* Leaders

2. G. Jones, "Coaching real leaders," *T&D Magazine*, August 2008, 34–37.

Safe Leaders	*Real* Leaders
• Are fearful of making mistakes because of the implications these might have for their job security	• See mistakes as a key part of their development and learning
• Look to blame others when things go wrong	• Accept responsibility and accountability when things go wrong
• Respond to failure by sweeping it under the carpet	• Are courageous in seeking to understand the causes of failure
• Claim successes as their own	• Recognize others' contributions to successes
• View challenge as unhelpful and threatening	• Encourage challenge and collective problem-solving
• Hide behind bureaucracy	• Are willing to take calculated risks to reach stretching goals
• Hide behind resource/capacity constraints	• Create innovative opportunities
• Encourage conformity to "tried and tested" methods	• Encourage people to challenge accepted ways of thinking and acting
• Dismiss others' suggestions for change	• Cultivate creativity
• Pay lip service to change initiatives	• Lead by example through driving change
• Insist on their people's compliance	• Inspire their people's commitment
• Avoid dealing with the real issues	• Tackle issues head-on
• Settle for good rather than pushing for great	• Challenge themselves and others to raise the performance bar
• Are reluctant and slow to tackle underperformance	• Address underperformance when it arises
• Do not challenge or question those in positions of authority	• Ask the difficult questions of those above
• Wait to see what the majority think before speaking up	• Let people know what they think, irrespective of others' views
• Claim a "messenger" role in communicating tough decisions	• Make and own tough decisions
• Are out to please everyone	• Are willing to make decisions they know will be unpopular

Table 2.1 Key Differences Between *Safe* and *Real* Leaders, *continued*

Of course, *safe* leaders exist in various guises so that different people will exhibit the traits in varying degrees. What is common among them is their reluctance to put themselves on the line; they have too much to lose if they get it wrong.

- I worked with one *safe* leader whose "motive" was noticeable by his resistance to identify a vision and a long-term strategy and plan for the organization he headed up. He chose instead to keep himself busy by reacting to the usual day-to-day "trivia" which kept him out of any firing line.

- In another case, a business unit head clearly hid behind an overt claim that her style was to lead through consensus. This led to too much debate and conflict among her team of opinionated, strong-willed, and competitive individuals. She was too slow to make the decisions that needed to be made. She was playing it safe.

- Another *safe* leader of a large team lacked the courage to address underperformance. He was out to please everyone around him and claimed to be playing a "messenger" role in communicating any tough decisions. I was brought in as the "bad guy" who would do his dirty deeds for him. I did not work with him for very long!

Real leaders also come in different shapes and sizes.

- One female managing director of a large distribution company was very clear about her nonnegotiables when it came to providing quality customer service. This meant introducing metrics that would highlight areas of weakness and be unpopular with some of her people because they were at risk of being exposed as underperformers. And not all members of her board agreed with her either, but she was resolute in her rationale and the new metrics resulted in a significant impact on customer satisfaction. Here was a *real* leader who was willing to challenge the status quo despite the fact it was not popular to begin with.

• A president of a well-known company was instrumental in bringing about a much-needed culture change in the organization through *real* leadership in the form of clear role-modeling of values that would underpin future success. The culture had been characterized by hard work and very long working hours. He recognized that the future well-being of the company depended on working smarter, not harder. At least once a week, he would make a big thing of leaving the office early, saying that he was going home to spend some quality time with his family.

• Finally, I witnessed a managing director of a professional services company bring about a sharp increase in performance in an organization that was already performing well. The managing director thought that performance could actually be significantly better and that employees were not stretching themselves. She had a choice to make. She could either play it safe and oversee the continued success of the organization and enjoy her popularity when it came to bonus time, or she could challenge her people to stretch themselves and achieve their true potential. She chose the *real* leader option and started to communicate her thoughts around how she thought the future of the organization was threatened by a complacency that was becoming ever more apparent. Her calls for everyone to raise the performance bar were met with derision, but they became the foundation of the company's step change to the next performance level.

Real and *Safe* Leadership During Turbulent Times

The differences between *real* and *safe* leaders are particularly pronounced during tough and turbulent times for organizations. Remember that what lies at the core of *safe* leaders will mainly be about role security. These leaders really value the prestige, status, power, authority, and the financial package that come with leadership. There is a lot to lose, so much so that, particularly in tough times, their main focus will be staying out of the firing line and becoming even more risk-averse; not taking risks, to them, means ensuring no mistakes. They withdraw into a safety zone. Now is the time to avoid conflict, and it becomes too risky to challenge peers' or bosses' views. They spend less time coaching their people and more time telling their subordinates what to do and how to do it. They are careful what they say and sit tight in the hope that more favorable times are just around the corner. Their focus is on cutting costs and hitting short-term targets.

At the other end of this continuum is the *real* leader. Remember that these leaders are driven mainly by the challenge and opportunity to put themselves out there, make a difference, and have a real impact. Tough times are their calling; they come to the fore and are even more highly visible. They focus on what they can control and make things happen. *Real* leaders make and stand by their decisions and "tell it how it is." They view a tough economic climate as a time when development is most needed; this is the time to nurture and retain talent in order to gain competitive advantage in the longer term. Their skills are probably even more prominent as they strive to lead their organization and support their people through turbulent, sometimes catastrophic, circumstances. This is where their personal resources are so important, to the extent that they unwittingly or perhaps deliberately expose them to their people: Their resilience, optimism balanced with realism, strength of character, vast experience, care, and determination will be very evident. But so, too, will the fact that they are human beings like everyone else. They also have doubts and worries, and there is no point in hiding them. *Real* leaders are authentic, and their impact in organizations is much more a function of *how they are* than *what they do*.

What Type of Leader Are *You*?

I have highlighted the extremes of *real* and *safe* leadership in order to demonstrate the key differences between them. The likelihood, of course, is that most leaders will sit somewhere along the continuum of *real* and *safe* leader motives. Use Time-Out 2 to figure out your own motives to lead and where *you* lie on the continuum.

TIME-OUT 2

WHAT TYPE OF LEADER ARE *YOU*?

What are your motives to be a leader? Is it about the status, package, power, and authority that come with the role? Is it the accountability and vision required that attract you? Or is it about the opportunity to make a difference and have a *real* impact? Where do you sit along the *real-safe* leader motives continuum?

The Remainder of This Book Is About *You*!

Now that you know what *real* leaders are, the following chapter moves on to examine their purpose in terms of their specific role within organizations. Since you are reading this with the clear intention of operating as a *real* leader, from now on this book is about *you*.

KEY TAKEAWAYS

■ *Safe* leaders are unwilling to put themselves on the line and do everything they can to stay out of the firing line.

■ *Real* leaders are driven by the challenge and the opportunity to make a difference and have a positive impact on their people.

■ *Real* leaders' impact is a function of *how they are* rather than *what they do*.

Chapter 3

■ ■ ■

Real Leaders Focus on Creating High-Performance Environments

KEY TOPICS

■ How *real* leaders create high-performance environments
■ The strategic focus of *real* leaders
■ Vision, support, and challenge behaviors

This chapter describes how *real* leaders focus on creating environments where high performance is inevitable and sustainable. It concludes with the proposition that the accountability that comes with assuming this role requires *real* leaders to be mentally tough.

Delivering High Performance That Is Inevitable and Sustainable

At the end of the day, you as a leader are only ever measured on one thing: performance. Inspiring people to follow you is insufficient to satisfy key stakeholders and keep you in your job if it is not accompanied by performance returns. At the same time, short-term performance gains are no good if they are not deliverable year in, year out. Your role as a leader, therefore, is to create an environment where high performance is both inevitable and sustainable.[3] As a *real* leader, you must recognize that you are not a "true" performer any longer, and that your task is to create the conditions where the people who *are* delivering the bottom line are able to thrive with as few constraints and as much support as possible. This will require some courage on your part because you must have confidence and trust in your people to deliver.

You, as a *real* leader, are at the core of this environment, and your task is to ensure that carefully selected performers with a variety of talents and skills appropriate to the different roles they play are inspired to produce a clearly defined and communicated output. As such, you are not "doing" the performance yourself; instead, you have the crucial role of making sure the right people are in the right roles, that they all know what is expected of them, and that they understand how their individual inputs contribute to the total output. You must ensure synchrony and a collective commitment to producing the best performance possible day after day. First, however, you must determine the strategic focus of your organization, business unit, and/or team that will drive the mindsets and behaviors of your people.

Getting the Strategic Focus Right

Getting the strategic focus right is vital in any environment where high performance is inevitable and sustainable. Where you direct your focus is critical because it is a limited resource—you only have so much of it! In this way, leadership can be thought of as involving the management of two dynamic tensions[4] which represent factors in the environment that compete for your attention.

3. The research team at Lane4 has identified the key components of environments that deliver high performance that is both inevitable and sustainable. This has involved searching and making sense of a huge scientific literature and drawing out the factors shown to affect bottom-line performance. We have also conducted studies to validate the resulting framework as it has evolved. This work has been published; see note 6 on page 32.
4. Based on R. E. Quinn and J. Rohrbaugh, "A competing values approach to organizational effectiveness," *Public Productivity Review*, 1981, 5, 122–140.

1. A "current" versus "future" tension. A "current" focus involves attending to the short-term performance, efficiency, and stability of the organization. A "future" focus involves attending to longer-term stability, flexibility, and change initiatives. A strong focus on the "current" means that there is little focus left for the "future," and vice versa.

2. An "internal" versus "external" tension. An "internal" focus is largely on organizational capability through its people, systems, and processes. An "external" focus is directed toward stakeholder demands, competitive position, and differentiation in the marketplace. A strong "internal" focus means that there is little focus left for the "external" end of the continuum, and vice versa.

But what should the "specific" areas of strategic focus be when managing these tensions? Figure 3.1 illustrates the two dynamic tensions along with the factors in the quadrants that have been shown in scientific research[5] to determine bottom-line business performance: achievement, internal processes, innovation, and well-being.

- **Achievement.** This current and external focus is about delivering against short-term goals, typically in the form of revenue and profit. My experience is that there is a huge emphasis on this in the retail sector where short-term revenue generation is so important.

- **Internal processes.** This current and internal focus is on the internal systems, processes, procedures, etc. that underpin the efficiency of organizations. Examples include

5. Based on M. G. Patterson, M. A. West, R. Lawthon, and S. Nickell, *Impact of People Management Practices on Business Performance*, Institute of Personnel and Development: London, 1997.

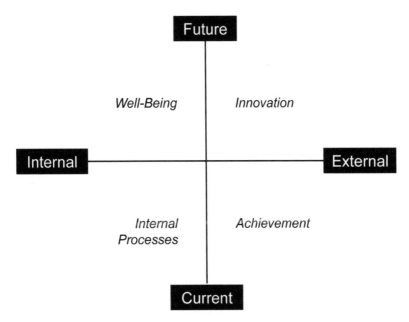

Figure 3.1 Dynamic Tensions and Determinants of Bottom-Line Performance

performance management systems and IT infrastructure. In my experience, government and public agencies have a very strong emphasis on this factor because many of them are typified by managing a huge amount and flow of information efficiently.

- **Innovation.** This future and external focus is largely on the marketplace and things like new products and marketing. The types of organizations I have worked with that have a heavy emphasis on market sector innovation include pharmaceuticals; they are incessantly trying to develop the next wonder drug.

- **Well-being.** This future and internal focus is about your people's level of commitment to the organization, their job satisfaction, and their trust in and loyalty to the leadership of the organization that is so vital to future growth. This factor often does not receive the focus it deserves, which is unfortunate since well-being is about the longer-term sustainability of performance. It enables organizations to retain their top talent and to grow their own people.

It is the relative degree of focus on these factors, and how the levels are balanced against each other, that is important.[6] Of particular relevance to this balance is the notion that a dominant focus on internal processes and achievement, rather than well-being and innovation, reflects a strong "current focus," which is very typical in tough times. Conversely, a dominant focus on innovation and well-being reflects a strong "future focus."

As shown in Figure 3.2, the safer option for leaders is to focus on the short term: hitting the numbers. This is what leaders are generally incentivized on; it is how stakeholders measure their performance. It is also "convenient" for *safe* leaders to focus on the short term because they are dragged into the functional detail and simply do not have enough time to focus on the future; at least, that is what they claim!

Real leaders, on the other hand, recognize their responsibility is to focus more on the longer term: innovation and, in particular, well-being. These are what the long-term health of the organization is dependent upon. High-performance organizations are in a constant state of formal or informal change. They can never stand still as they seek to maintain and extend their competitive advantage. This is where *real* leaders play such a crucial role. It is their above-the-line focus that will ensure continual progress onward and upward.

6. G. Jones, M. Gittins, and L. Hardy, "Creating an environment where high performance is inevitable and sustainable: The High Performance Environment Model," *Annual Review of High Performance Coaching and Consulting*, 2009, 139–149.

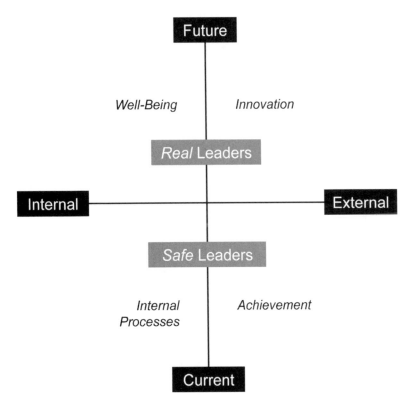

Figure 3.2 The Focus of *Real* and *Safe* Leaders

Even during tough times, *real* leaders make sure their focus is on the longer term because they are very aware that good times will return; they need to be equipped and prepared to take advantage when those times come. And this is where s*afe* leaders come unstuck; they will probably have stripped away so many costs in bad times, and also lost some of their best people through lack of development opportunities, that they find themselves underresourced and playing catch-up when the better times return.

Real Leaders Provide Vision, Challenge, *and* Support

Once you have everything in place, then your day-to-day role as a *real* leader, in its simplest form, is to remind your performers of the vision, challenge them to deliver their contribution to achieving it, and support them in doing so.[7] But what underpins vision, challenge, and support in *real* leaders?

- **Vision.** This is a central element of *real* leadership because it forms the link between strategy and people, whether it be for your organization, business unit, or functional team. It is the vehicle by which leaders are able to engage people's motivation and provide purpose, direction, and cohesion. But creating a compelling vision is not enough to inspire your people day in and day out. As a *real* leader, you must continually remind them of it and, even more important, role model it. If your vision emphasizes innovation in the marketplace, for example, then you must talk about how important innovation is and acknowledge and reward it when you come across it.

- **Challenge.** Visions should always challenge and stretch organizations and the people within them. Challenge can take many forms, some of them more constructive than others! As a *real* leader, the most effective challenge behaviors are to remind performers of the high expectations on them, thus challenging them to think about old problems and issues in new ways, and to encourage them to work collectively rather than on their own. Providing developmental feedback on areas for improving competence is a powerful tool for instilling accountability and responsibility in your team.

7. G. Jones, M. Gittins, and L. Hardy, "Creating an environment where high performance is inevitable and sustainable: The High Performance Environment Model," *Annual Review of High Performance Coaching and Consulting*, 2009, 139–149.

Challenge is about moving people out of their comfort zone and opening them to experiences that will test and develop their capabilities. Through appropriate challenge, leaders communicate performance excellence, set stretching goals, and foster innovation and adaptability.

- **Support.** Although high challenge is a critical element of high performance, without support it creates a sink-or-swim scenario. To ensure that performance is sustainable over the longer term, a *real* leader's challenge needs to be complemented by support behaviors. Through appropriate support, leaders promote learning and build trust among their respective followers. Your people are like all normal human beings: they want to be told when they are doing a good job. Motivational feedback in the form of encouragement will support them in reinforcing what is expected of them and help to maintain their confidence and motivation. They also want you to know them as individuals and to provide them with the specific individual support they desire. Realizing that individuals want you to take a personal interest in them will earn considerable loyalty and commitment among them.

Table 3.1, on the following page, shows the impact of demonstrating vision, challenge, *and* support behaviors. It also shows how *not* engaging in all three behaviors determines leadership style. Specifically, this table describes how different combinations of imbalance across the three behaviors determine different styles of leadership.

The characteristics of the environments created by the various combinations of vision, challenge, and support provided by leaders are described below.

Vision	Challenge	Support	Leadership Is . . .
√	√	√	Real
√	√	X	Relentless
√	X	X	Pipe dream
√	X	√	Lacking edge
X	X	√	Polite
X	√	X	In your face
X	√	√	Rudderless
X	X	X	Safe

√ = Present   X = Absent

Table 3.1 Vision, Challenge, Support, and Leadership

Real leadership creates an environment where:

- Vision, challenge, and support are all evident and appropriately balanced, resulting in supportive challenge toward a clearly defined vision.

- Individuals and teams are clear about what is expected of them on a day-to-day basis as well in the longer term.

- Success is recognized and celebrated.

- People thrive in conditions created by the combination of high-performance expectations accompanied by high levels of support to achieve them.

- Coaching is the norm, being underpinned by good working relationships, a feedback culture, accountability and ownership, and clearly defined goals.

- There is a "we're in it together" mentality that is the foundation of high-performing teams.

- "Healthy competition" exists in the form of shared learning and commitment to everyone's development, as well as individual and team goals being completely aligned.

A *real* leader devotes a large proportion of his or her time to coaching, giving and receiving feedback, and consulting with others to understand the current challenges. This leader communicates with people personally to congratulate them on their successes; regular formal and informal performance reviews are held to clarify expectations and monitor progress.

Relentless leadership creates an environment where:

- Individuals and teams are continually reminded of the vision and there is plenty of challenge to deliver it, but little support.

- The lack of support accompanied by high challenge results in a "sink or swim" environment that breeds an "I'm on my own" mentality.

- High performance is likely but is probably not sustainable because of stress and potential burnout.

- There is likely to be a blame culture that becomes evident when the high standards are not achieved.

- Recognition for good performance is likely to be rare because it is expected.

- There is little care for well-being, resulting in many people feeling uncomfortable and under the spotlight.

A *relentless* leader demands that league tables of individuals' sales performances are posted on the walls of the call center. At meetings, this leader exposes and ridicules those at the bottom of the table, reminding them about how they are letting their colleagues down and not contributing to the company's future success. The *relentless* leader threatens underperformers with a "shape up or ship out" ultimatum. There is no time to celebrate successes because of the *relentless* leader's constant drive toward the next higher, faster, bigger targets.

Pipe dream leadership creates an environment where:

- The vision is talked about regularly but is nothing more than a pipe dream because of the lack of challenge and support.

- There are no plans in place for how the vision will be achieved.

- The leader lacks credibility.

- There is a lack of goals so that individuals are unclear about expectations.

- The culture is one of mediocrity.

- There is an "I don't know what I'm supposed to be doing" mentality.

A *pipe dream* leader holds lots of vision meetings, has mugs made up with the company logo and motto on them, and talks grandly about what is going to happen next quarter and next year. This leader makes vague promises about his or her company leading the digital revolution, yet provides no concrete goals for the employees to work toward.

Lacking edge leadership creates an environment where:

- There is a vision and plenty of support available, but little in the way of challenge.

- Underperformance is not addressed.

- It is too cozy and individuals are working within their comfort zones.

- There is little sense and celebration of achievement because it is not valued highly.

- It can be stifling for individuals who want to be stretched.

- There is an "out to please" mentality.

A *lacking edge* leader talks passionately about the future and how the organization is lucky to have such a great bunch of people who will achieve it. This leader avoids conflict, leaves underperformance to be addressed by someone else, and basks in being told how good things are.

Polite leadership creates an environment where:

- The lack of vision and challenge means there is no direction.

- The high support and the absence of challenge can create an overly caring, parentlike culture.

- Ambiguity and uncertainty abound because individuals are unsure what is expected of them in the short term, and they are also unsure where they are headed.

- There is an air of complacency.

- People are bored.

- There is an "I'm safe as long as I keep my head down" mentality.

A *polite* leader enquires about peoples' families on regular office walkabouts. This leader talks constantly about having a "nice" culture with "nice" people and "how well" the organization is doing. Employees' questions about the direction of the organization and the objectives over the next one or two years and beyond are met with vague and, often, contradictory statements.

In your face leadership creates an environment where:

- Pressure is high because the emphasis on short-term performance is combined with the lack of support and a vision.

- There is potential conflict among individuals and teams because of the short-term urgency to produce results.

- People do not feel valued because they are unsure how the performance demanded from them contributes to the future of the organization.

- The short-term performance focus can result in micromanagement.

- "Unhealthy competition" exists in the form of a lack of willingness to work effectively in teams because the "big picture" is unclear, failing to share best practice, and a focus on "beating" colleagues at any cost.

- An "avoidance" mentality exists because of the consequences of failing or making mistakes.

An *in your face* leader phones key people every day to check on the previous day's numbers and cannot resist suggesting ways of doing things differently and, typically, "my way." This leader continually reminds people of only the very small number of people who will make it on to the "all expenses paid plus spending money" trip to Las Vegas at the end of the quarter.

Rudderless leadership creates an environment where:

- There is lots of challenge and support, but nobody knows what the vision is.

- The focus is on short-term performance, but the pressure is alleviated by the high support available.

- The high challenge *and* high support result in a focus on inspiring people to deliver more.

- The culture is one of "busyness"; there is plenty going on.

- Silos exist because the lack of a vision means teams do not have an overt reason for working together effectively.

- There is an "I'm not sure why I'm working so hard" mentality.

A *rudderless* leader is very busy tackling day-to-day issues as they arise and holds lots of one-on-ones with team members to drill down into progress toward short-term goals and the support they require to achieve them. This leader sometimes apologizes about the stretching goals that are set and how his or her door is always open to people who are struggling and need help.

Safe leadership creates an environment where:

- There appears to be little going on; the environment is stagnant.

- There is a strong sense of politics.

- It is more about *who* you know than *what* you know.

- People are not stimulated.

- A lot happens behind closed doors.

- There is little respect for the leaders.

- Good performance happens more by accident than by design.

- There is an "I don't care" mentality.

A *safe* leader is simply too busy to have time to focus on the future. This leader avoids challenge and therefore holds meetings with a chosen few, reminds people about the company line on how to do things, and apologizes for unpopular and controversial decisions passed down from on high. He or she communicates a lot of information from above, being careful not to share his or her opinion or take responsibility for any decisions made. This leader also has regular lunches with carefully chosen peers and senior leaders who are influential.

The undesirable nature of the various imbalances across vision, challenge, and support emphasizes the importance of focusing on and practicing all three behaviors to be a *real* leader. Focusing on demonstrating vision, challenge, *and* support behaviors can result in significant and sustained performance gains. These behaviors, in combination, can unleash the performance potential of people by providing them with an environment where they can thrive. Environments not conducive to high performance that is inevitable and sustainable are created by leaders who anchor themselves in one or two areas to the exclusion of the other(s).

Do *You* Provide Vision, Challenge, *and* Support?

So where do *you* feature among the different types of leadership described in the previous section? Where do you think your direct reports would place you? Have you got some work to do? Spend a few minutes reflecting on the questions in Time-Out 3.

TIME-OUT 3

DO *YOU* PROVIDE VISION, CHALLENGE, *AND* SUPPORT?

What is your vision for your organization, business unit, and/or team? How often do you talk about it?

To what extent do you challenge your people? What form does this take?

To what extent do you provide support to your people? What form does this take?

Have you got the balance right?

So Are You Still Willing to Put Yourself on the Line?

I began this book by asking if you are willing to put yourself on the line as a leader. Now you know why I asked the question. Being a *real* leader is very demanding and can be tough. The expectations and pressure are unrelenting. There is no hiding place! That is where mental toughness is critical.

KEY TAKEAWAYS

- *Real* leaders focus on creating environments where high performance is inevitable and sustainable; their focus is more on the future than the current.
- *Real* leaders provide balanced vision, challenge, and support.
- *Real* leaders step up to the plate in turbulent times.
- *Real* leaders need to be mentally tough.

Chapter 4

■ ■ ■

Real Leadership, Pressure, and Mental Toughness

KEY TOPICS

■ What pressure is, and its different sources
■ How pressure can either facilitate or debilitate your performance
■ The four key skills of mental toughness

My work with *real* leaders at the core of mergers, acquisitions, redundancies, management buyouts, and companies going public has equipped me with a fascinating insight into the enormous pressure that can make or break them. These are the situations in which leaders struggle and sometimes fold under pressure—or thrive on it. As a *real* leader, whether it be major events or the incessant daily demands of creating and maintaining an environment where high-level performance is inevitable and sustainable, pressure surrounds you and sometimes consumes you.

Where Does Pressure Come From?

The pressure that comes with being a *real* leader is understood most simply in the context of the relationship between yourself and the environment in which you lead.

The Environment

The environment is where the most obvious and common sources of pressure exist. These are the pressures imposed on you (see Figure 4.1), such as delivering short-term results, building a strategy for growth, making the tough decisions that come your way, direct reports' demands on your time, uncertainty, and constant change. Externally imposed pressures like these are often accepted as "part of the territory," and will increase as you climb the corporate ladder. Indeed, research has shown that job promotions increase pressure on average by 10 percent.[8]

External pressure for *real* leaders comes in two forms. The first stems from those demands that are highly visible within the organization, such as delivering the expected growth and profit numbers and reporting them at stakeholder meetings, delivering impactful

Pressure

Figure 4.1 Pressure Comes from the Environment

8. C. Boyce and A. Oswald, "Do people become healthier after being promoted?" *Discussion Paper Number 3894*, Institute of Labor, University of Warwick, December 2008.

presentations, and inspiring people with a compelling vision. The second form of external pressure arises from those less visible, more "localized" day-to-day demands that are expected of *real* leaders. Examples include making time for individuals, carrying out performance reviews, and leading by example.

Yourself

There is another source of pressure that is not quite so obvious—yourself! Much of the pressure you experience in the workplace will come from others' expectations of you, but this is often exacerbated by heaping even greater expectations on yourself. Self-imposed pressure comes in two forms:

1. Pressure that you actively seek in the external environment (see Figure 4.2). Many people seek pressures that make their day-to-day existence more interesting and challenging.

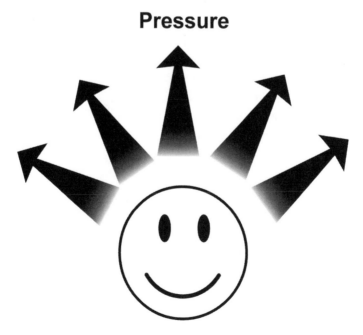

Pressure

Figure 4.2 Seeking Pressure in the Environment

These will vary enormously among leaders but can include setting yourself stretching goals, aspiring to the next promotion, studying part time for that next qualification, etc. Pressure in this form results from choices you have made about how you want to lead and the type of leader you want to be. Your choice to be a *real* rather than a *safe* leader is made in the knowledge that you will be highly visible and is, therefore, something you impose on yourself. And in this role, you will probably want to exceed the organization's and colleagues' expectations of you. Because these are *your* expectations of yourself and do not originate from the external environment, you are imposing pressure on yourself. And simple things such as saying "yes" to everyone's requests of you will ensure that self-imposed pressure mounts. Do not blame the people making the requests for the increased pressure on you and your time—blame yourself!

2. Unfortunately, you seldom seem to have control over the second type of self-imposed pressure. It is that cunning form that occupies your head (see Figure 4.3). This is the potential monster that plays games with your mind and creates pressure when it should not exist. It taunts your conscience and distorts your perceptions. It sees problems when there are none. It turns small challenges into big issues. It creates enormous expectations of yourself that others do not have. It focuses your attention on the one member of your team

Figure 4.3 The Pressure Inside Your Head

who looks disinterested in your presentation rather than on the remaining nine who are totally engaged. It may challenge your conscience that you made a mistake in deciding to let that underperformer go. Worse still, it may cause you to want to prove yourself to those small few who you have assumed do not respect you as a leader because they have never actually told you they are happy with your leadership.

Whatever its source, pressure can bring out the best and the worst in all of us. At its worst, it makes being a leader miserable and stressful. At its best, pressure enriches your existence as a leader, making it fulfilling and meaningful, inspiring you to higher, and even extraordinary, levels of performance. How pressure affects you is largely your own choice. It may not seem like it sometimes, but you do not have to be stressed and debilitated by pressure. In fact, you can positively thrive on it through being mentally tough.

Mental Toughness

Mental toughness enables *real* leaders to thrive on pressure. More than ability, experience, and education, in today's fast-moving, highly competitive world, it is mental toughness that will determine who succeeds and who fails. Mental toughness helps you to:

- Bounce back after setbacks

- Maintain belief in yourself when doubts are gnawing away at you

- Remain focused in the face of numerous distractions

- Keep going when all seems lost

- Turn threats into opportunities

- Find ways of motivating yourself when you are struggling to keep going

- Harness thoughts and feelings so they work *for* you rather than *against* you

- Make choices when there appear to be none available

- Remain in control

The good news is that mental toughness can be developed so that you, too, can learn to cope with and actually thrive on pressure.

The Four Key Skills of Mental Toughness

The portrayal of mental toughness shown in Figure 4.4, on the following page, was originally generated from studies[9, 10] carried out by Professor Sheldon Hanton, Dr. Declan Connaughton, and myself. These studies involved asking elite athletes about their own mental toughness, and also how it manifested in other elite athletes whom they considered to be particularly mentally tough. The athletes defined mental toughness as the ability to perform at consistently high levels in pressure situations. These findings have been replicated in our follow-up studies of high performers from different industry sectors in the business world. For example, high-performing equity traders in a large global bank defined mental toughness as "the ability to perform at consistently high levels through times of personal and professional pressure." In another study, a group of high-performing salespeople in a market research company defined mental toughness as "the ability to respond positively to multiple and sometimes conflicting pressures and deliver consistently successful performance."

9. G. Jones, S. Hanton, and D. Connaughton, "What is this thing called mental toughness? An investigation of elite performers," *Journal of Applied Sport Psychology,* 2002, 14, 205–218.
10. ———, "A framework of mental toughness in the world's best performers," *The Sport Psychologist,* 2007, 21, 243–264.

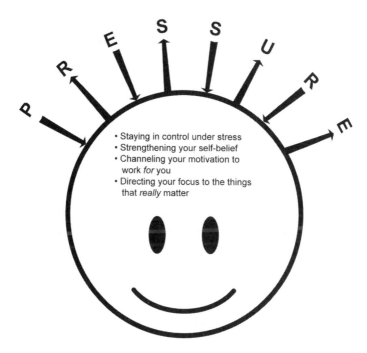

Figure 4.4 The Four Key Skills of Mental Toughness

These studies show unequivocally that mental toughness is about performing to consistently high levels when under pressure, and it is the same in sports and business. The studies also show that mental toughness is underpinned by the ability to control stress, motivation, self-belief, and focus when under pressure.

So mental toughness comprises four key skills that *real* leaders are able to instantly identify with as enabling them to sustain high levels of performance in their pressured environments. My experience of working, originally with elite athletes, and more recently with *real* leaders has enabled me to pinpoint the key essentials of employing these skills successfully. Specifically, these skills can be used to stay in control under stress, strengthen your self-belief, channel your motivation to work *for* you, and direct your focus to the things that *really* matter. They can be thought of as follows:

- **Staying in control under stress.** This skill is important when the pressures of being a *real* leader become so overwhelming they spill over to cause stress, that negative and potentially debilitating state. This skill enables you to control the amount and nature of the stress you are under so that you can remain composed when you are weighing up situations and making important decisions.

- **Strengthening your self-belief.** The high visibility and accountability associated with being a *real* leader, particularly during challenging times, may make you feel vulnerable. This skill strengthens your belief and confidence in your qualities and abilities as a *real* leader in order to take on the challenges ahead.

- **Channeling your motivation to work *for* you.** This skill ensures that your determination to succeed as a *real* leader is founded on positive and constructive motives that keep you optimally motivated and enable you to recover from setbacks and failures.

- **Directing your focus to the things that *really* matter.** As a *real* leader, there will be a multitude of demands on your time and energy that are a potential source of distraction. This skill enables you to identify your key priorities and responsibilities and then stay focused on them.

The sales force study I referred to earlier in this section compared people who were formally classified as "high performers" in the organization with peers who were classified as "average performers." The "high performers" scored higher on all four of the mental toughness key skills than their peers, showing that they really do make a difference in delivering sustainable high performance.

How Mentally Tough Are *You*?

So there it is. You are now familiar with the key skills of mental toughness. Spend a few minutes reflecting on the questions in Time-Out 4. This will provide an indication of how mentally tough *you* are.

TIME-OUT 4

HOW MENTALLY TOUGH ARE *YOU*?

How does stress affect you? Are you able to remain composed so that you are able to make important decisions?

Are you able to maintain belief in yourself when the pressure is on and things are going wrong?

Do you bounce back after setbacks because of your determination to succeed?

What happens to your focus when you are under pressure? Are you able to stay focused on key priorities, or do you get distracted by things outside your control?

Whatever your current level of mental toughness, you will benefit from building on it further. It will form the foundation of your ability to thrive on the pressure of being a *real* leader.

KEY TAKEAWAYS

■ **Pressure assumes at least two forms: pressure that is externally imposed and pressure that is self-**

continued

imposed by either actively seeking it in the environment or through creating it within your own mind.
■ Pressure can either facilitate or debilitate performance, depending on how you respond to it.
■ Mental toughness can be developed.
■ Mental toughness enables you to cope with and
even thrive on pressure.
■ Mental toughness comprises four key skills that
form the foundation of sustained high performance: staying in control under stress, channeling
your motivation to work *for* you, strengthening
your self-belief, and directing your focus to the
things that *really* matter.

That Concludes Master Class 1

This is the conclusion of Master Class 1 in which a considerable
amount of ground has been covered, including:

- The many demands on leaders and in particular the visibility and exposure that often come with the role

- The different motives that underpin the distinction between
  real and *safe* leaders and how these drive leader behaviors

- How *real* leaders create high-performance environments

- The key role of mental toughness in helping *real* leaders
  to thrive on pressure

The great news is that mental toughness can be developed. The
master classes that follow will introduce, and guide you through,
a variety of strategies and tools that will enable you to thrive on
the pressure of being a *real* leader.

Master Class 2

■■■

Staying in Control Under the Inevitable Stress That Comes with Being a *Real* Leader

OBJECTIVES

■ To help you identify the sources of your stress and how they affect you

■ To equip you with tools to help you control your stress symptoms

■ To guide you in recognizing and challenging the thinking that causes you stress

■ To enable you to take control over the situations and circumstances that cause you stress

■■■

Chapter 5

■■■

Stress: The Dark Side of Pressure

KEY TOPICS

■ **What stress is and how its affects you**
■ **How to recognize when you are *choosing* to be stressed**
■ **The different types of strategies and tools that will help you stay in control under stress**

Being a mentally tough *real* leader does not mean that you do not get stressed. After all, creating a high-performance environment is no easy task. Tackling issues such as underperformance head-on, making and owning tough decisions that you know will be unpopular, and at the same time keeping your people engaged and committed all bring with them a weight of responsibility and inevitable visibility that can sometimes overwhelm you.

The key to delivering sustained high performance under the spotlight that shines so brightly on *real* leaders is to develop strategies and tools that enable you to control stress so that important decisions can be thought out in a calm and composed manner. This master class addresses *how* you can control stress, but it is important to first establish what stress actually is, and then how pressure and stress are related.

The Two Faces of Pressure

The managing director of a large manufacturing company was announcing the plan, agreed on with the global CEO only the day before, to his expectant senior executive team. This was a plan designed to combat successive substantial, uncontrollable hikes in energy prices that had turned early-year forecasts of a healthy profit into a likely significant loss accompanied by plant closures. The next few days would be vital as the leaders around the table were tasked to act quickly to deliver difficult messages to their respective parts of the business. As the MD's coach who had also worked closely with the team, I was in the privileged position of observing this scenario unfold. As my gaze wandered around the faces of the leaders in the room, there were a couple whose frightened eyes, tension, and paleness signalled the inner angst that had so clearly risen to the surface. They were dreading the days to come. Some other faces portrayed a very different experience. There was a steely determination and eagerness to begin their task. For them, this was what the job was all about.

I have witnessed similar scenes in sport on numerous occasions during those final hours, minutes, and moments leading up to a big event. The faces, and particularly the eyes, of athletes are the windows to their minds. They reveal either an excitement and eagerness for the action to begin, or a frozen terror of what is about to unfold. This is the pressure cauldron that can determine the outcome before the contest has even begun. Such scenes represent the two "faces" of pressure shown in Figure 5.1, on the following page.

At its best, pressure energizes and invigorates leaders. It sharpens their focus and brings out the best in them. At its worst, pressure crushes and drains them. This negative side of pressure is otherwise known as "stress," that often unpleasant and debilitating consequence of not coping with pressure.

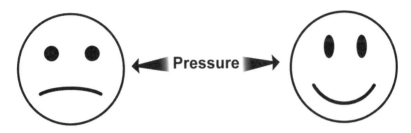

Figure 5.1 The Two Faces of Pressure

This master class focuses on the negative face of pressure that causes you stress. I have encountered stress in many different circumstances among business leaders. In the run-up to a company going public, for example, senior figures were working ridiculous hours to achieve what seemed like impossible targets in an effort to maximize share price. These people were certainly not thriving on the pressure! Stress was also a major factor for leaders in a large organization that experienced a yearlong period of uncertainty surrounding a much publicized takeover. The uncertainty, together with a lack of control, were the ingredients for widespread stress.

And imagine the stress experienced by senior leaders of investment banks at the height of the financial meltdown. One leader I worked with in a major Wall Street bank described having to make big decisions in the midst of a torrent of information that changed seemingly by the minute. She admitted to being clueless about what might happen next, describing it as "trying to manage a waterfall of uncertainty and anxiety." It was during this fateful time that I saw the extremes of uncertainty and lack of control, which I can only describe as "chaos" and "helplessness" respectively! This was some of the most severe stress I have ever witnessed in the commercial world.

Major events like those described above are not the only cause of stress in leaders. It can simply be the result of the daily grind, hassles, and sometimes the monotony of work getting on top of you. Or it can be a result of the incessant demands on you as a leader to drive change, challenge the status quo, and encourage your people to raise the bar that wear you down.

Stress and *You*

There are three essential requirements for tackling and controlling your stress:

- Identifying the sources of pressure that lead to stress, if you let them

- Recognizing when you *are* stressed

- Developing suitable strategies and tools for controlling your stress

The model[11] shown in Figure 5.2, on the following page, will form the foundation for your development in these three areas. It is a simple and practical way of viewing stress and its effects, leading to how to cope with it. The key components of the model, described in the following sections, are:

- *Your sources of pressure* that may lead to stress

- *Who you are* in terms of how you normally deal with pressure, and how this may contribute to causing you stress

- *Your choice about how to view and think about pressure* as either an "opportunity" or a "threat" and how this may result in stress

---

11. G. Jones, "Performance excellence: A personal perspective on the link between sport and business," *Journal of Applied Sport Psychology*, 2002, 14, 268–281.

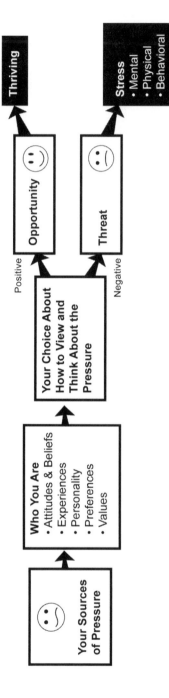

Figure 5.2 The Stress Process

- *Stress* and how it affects you mentally, physically, and behaviorally

Let's take a look at the model in action before you apply it to understand your own stress and how it affects you.

Imagine two different leaders, Max and Jenny, who have both reached a decision to confront a disruptive member of their team in the next team meeting. This is a source of pressure to both of them.

In each case, both have addressed the issue on a one-on-one basis, but the individual continues to be a disruptive influence. He is now an obstacle to running effective team meetings and is destabilizing team unity. Confronting the individual when he is being disruptive in a team setting is the only option left. The pressure is exacerbated by the fact that the person is bright, opinionated, and a high performer with a big ego.

Max is stressed by the anticipation of dealing with the individual in front of the team. He has witnessed this type of situation previously when his boss confronted a member of the team Max used to be a part of. His boss made the mistake of getting uncontrollably angry and was made to look stupid. Max is also an introvert and is frustrated by having to resolve the problem in a public forum. He gets tongue-tied when under stress and worries about being made to look foolish in front of his team. Max definitely views the situation as a threat to his reputation as the leader of the team and loses plenty of sleep as a result.

Jenny, on the other hand, is extremely values-driven, with one really important value being that people should respect authority. The disruptive team member's attitude and behavior are unacceptable within her belief system. Here is an opportunity to deal not only with the problem individual once and for all, but also to gain the respect of her team for challenging intolerable behavior no matter how good a performer he is. Jenny is definitely viewing this as an opportunity to enhance her reputation with the team and will approach it with plenty of her usual confidence.

So, here we have two leaders faced with the same pressure source who are viewing and reacting to it in very different ways. Underpinning their reactions are their different experiences, values, attitudes and beliefs, preferences, and personalities. Let's look at *your* sources of pressure and what it is about you that determines whether they cause you stress.

Your Sources of Pressure: The Pressure That Turns to Stress, If You Let It!

As I described in Chapter 4, pressure originates from two sources: yourself (internal) and the environment (external). I would like you to think about the pressure referred to in this part of the model as that which is imposed on you from the external environment in the form of the many demands on you as a *real* leader.

This will include the daily demands of things like providing "numbers updates" to challenging colleagues at meetings, or hitting those looming deadlines, or trying to present a positive demeanor to your people when things are going seriously wrong behind the scenes. Then there are the more major sources of pressure such as delivering important presentations, negotiating those crucial deals, or making those really tough decisions. Think about those sources of pressure that are especially relevant to you in your role as a *real* leader.

Who You Are—Are You Your Own Worst Enemy?

This part of the model is largely about your own tendency to impose pressure on yourself, which may then turn into stress. How do you normally deal with the pressures of *real* leadership and potentially stressful situations such as:

- Delivering negative feedback to an underperformer whom you have an uneasy relationship with?

- Chairing a big meeting of key stakeholders?

- Preparing to communicate a decision you know will be unpopular?

The way you respond in these types of situations will be the function of a number of things about "who you are." Particularly significant are:

- **Your attitudes and beliefs.** These relate to how you think and feel about the sources of pressure. You may enjoy and look forward to addressing underperformance, chairing important meetings, or communicating tough decisions because you are very good at it, or because of the buzz you get from the excitement of the adrenaline rush. Or you believe it is a necessary part of *real* leadership, so you should just accept and get on with it. On the other hand, these particular demands on you as a leader may be something you dread. This could be because you perceive yourself to be unable to perform at your best, or perhaps because you do not enjoy and are debilitated by the nerves you experience beforehand.

- **Your past experiences.** This refers to the previous occasions when you have addressed underperformance with individuals, the big meetings you have chaired, or the tough decisions you have communicated. How you dealt with the nerves, any feedback you received, and your own perceptions of how you performed will all be important. In this way, your past experiences will, to some extent, determine how you feel about upcoming similar situations. For example, if you have addressed underperformance with a specific direct report on a previous occasion, then how you feel about the upcoming feedback session with the same direct report will inevitably be strongly related to how it went with him or her in the past.

- **Your personality.** The personality formed in your early years is the one you have, relatively unchanged, throughout your life. This does not mean you have to think or behave in the same way forever; indeed, the development of mental toughness is based on the potential to be able to change thoughts and behavior. It does mean however that you are hardwired to respond in certain ways across different situations, and especially in high-pressure situations where your personality traits are likely to come to the fore. There are three dimensions of personality that are especially important in how you respond to pressure.

  - **Anxiety proneness:** This simply reflects the level of proneness to become anxious across a variety of situations. *Real* leaders who are high on anxiety proneness are likely to become anxious in most situations involving any pressure.

  - **Optimism-pessimism:** This dimension of personality speaks for itself. *Real* leaders who are high on optimism are likely to be more positive about coping with and performing well under pressure than those who are relative pessimists. Consequently, *real* leaders who are pessimists are more prone to experience stress than their more optimistic counterparts.

  - **Perfectionism:** For *real* leaders who are high on perfectionism, the need to do things perfectly adds even more pressure, making them more prone to experience stress than leaders who are not as high on perfectionism.

- **Your preferences.** As you have developed and matured as a person, you will have found ways of doing things that work for you. These will have turned into preferences that have become your natural way of leading your life, and you will take these into your role as a *real* leader. Some typical preferences that are evident in the workplace include:

- Working with detail versus thinking about the big picture

- Taking risks versus opting for the tried and tested methods

- Making decisions quickly versus taking the time to reflect

- Making decisions based on sound logic versus intuition and gut feel

- Wanting closure on decisions versus leaving them open

- Finishing projects well within the deadline versus last-minute completion

- Communicating via e-mail versus face-to-face

- Detailed planning and preparation versus a "let's see what happens" approach

- Working in teams and groups versus working on your own

Do you have any strong preferences from the list above? Working counter to your strong preferences takes you out of your comfort zone and can be stressful.

- **Your values.** You will have core values that reflect who you are and what you stand for. Values are not about what is right or wrong in the broad moral sense, but about what is right and wrong for you. If you find yourself in an environment where, for whatever reasons, you are unable to honor those values, you are likely to become frustrated and unhappy. If "hard work" and "excellence" are two of your core values, for example, and you work alongside colleagues who get by with doing the bare minimum and settle for mediocrity, then you are very likely to become stressed. What are your core values? As a *real* leader, are you living them out and standing behind them and making decisions based on them? Are your values aligned with your organization's values? Or is there a conflict so that you are having to compromise?

So what are the things about "who you are" that influence how you respond to the pressures that come with being a *real* leader? How do they influence the way you respond to the pressure sources that came to mind when reading the "Your Sources of Pressure" section?

Your Choice About How to View and Think About the Pressure—Do You Choose to Be Stressed?

Most stress is self-imposed! How you think about the pressure that comes with being a *real* leader determines whether you are stressed by it. The basic choice you have is between viewing the pressure as either positive in terms of providing an opportunity for you to thrive, or negative in that it poses a threat that results in stress and feeling anxious.

As you discovered in the previous section, "who you are" means that you have biases in your perception and interpretation of situations. For example, if you are high on anxiety proneness, you will have a tendency to naturally view most pressure as involving some threat. If you tend toward pessimism, you are likely to approach pressure situations anticipating that you will underperform, a biased appraisal that inevitably causes stress. And put pessimism together with high perfectionism, and you must perform perfectly, but you also believe you never will!

This realization that you have a choice about how you think about pressure is the first crucial step in controlling stress. The second is being aware of how "who you are" affects how you experience stress and the impact that has on how you view and approach it. Think about your sources of pressure as a *real* leader and how "who you are" influences your "choice" to be stressed by them or not.

Stress—How Does It Affect You?

When you are stressed, you are likely to experience symptoms that fall into three broad categories:

- **Mental** symptoms include things like doubt, worry, anger, feeling gloomy, poor memory recall, an inability to concentrate, frustration, feeling mentally drained, confusion, and panic. These are the symptoms that cloud your judgment when you are trying to make the right decisions. These are the symptoms that might slow you down when urgent conclusions need to be drawn. They often lurk in the form of distorted, negative perceptions that make things worse.

- **Physical** symptoms are those bodily reactions that can be quite unpleasant: the headache, those Jell-O legs, the sometimes uncomfortable muscle tension, the pounding heart, that tight chest, fast and shallow breathing, that feeling of sickness, the butterflies; or perhaps the empty feeling in the pit of your stomach, the sweaty palms, the voice tremor, and sometimes uncontrollable muscles in your face that betray the nerves, anger, or frustration you are trying so desperately to hide from your colleagues.

- **Behavioral** symptoms include fidgeting, pacing, verbal and physical aggression, crying, becoming quiet and withdrawn or maybe loud and outgoing, being short-tempered, indecisive, drinking excessive amounts of caffeine and alcohol, and disturbed sleep.

Do you recognize any of these symptoms in yourself? Work on identifying changes in your thoughts, bodily responses, and behavior when you are stressed. You might want to ask someone who knows you well to help you pinpoint behavioral changes and when they occur. In particular, think about your symptoms in response to the stress you experience as a *real* leader. This will alert you to when you are becoming stressed and the need to take action to control it.

You and Stress in a Nutshell

So far, this chapter has guided you through a series of steps that will help you satisfy two of the three essential requirements for controlling stress. First, you have reflected on the sources of pressure that can lead to stress, if you let them. Second, you have thought about what happens to you when you are stressed. Before moving on to the third essential requirement, developing strategies and tools for controlling your stress, spend a few minutes making sense of your reflections in Time-Out 5.

TIME-OUT 5

YOU AND STRESS IN A NUTSHELL

YOUR SOURCES OF PRESSURE

- **What pressures are you particularly conscious of, and how are they linked to any stress you experience?**

WHO YOU ARE

- **What are the things about you (personality, past experiences, attitudes, beliefs, preferences,**

values) that influence how you respond to the
pressures that come with being a *real* leader?

- How do they influence how you respond to the
  various pressures you identified above?

*THE CHOICE YOU HAVE ABOUT HOW YOU VIEW AND
THINK ABOUT THE PRESSURE*

- Reflecting back on your sources of pressure
  and the things about you that influence how you
  respond, what are your ways of thinking that
  cause you stress?

STRESS

- What mental, physical, and behavioral symptoms
  are you aware of when you are stressed?

Three Strategies for Staying in Control Under Stress

In the same way that you almost always have a choice over
whether to be stressed or not, so you also have a choice over how
to cope when you *are* stressed. There are three types of strategies and tools for controlling stress, shown in Figure 5.3: keeping
your stress symptoms under control, challenging the thinking that
causes you stress, and tackling the sources of your stress.

Mental toughness involves developing and enhancing all three
types of strategies:

1. Learning how to keep your stress symptoms under control will enable you to compose yourself at times when you are in danger of feeling overwhelmed.

2. Developing ways of challenging the thinking that causes you stress will help you keep things in perspective when your thoughts are beginning to run away with you.

3. Ultimately, it is in tackling the sources of your stress that will have the biggest impact in enabling you to thrive on pressure.

The remaining three chapters in this master class address each of these strategies in turn.

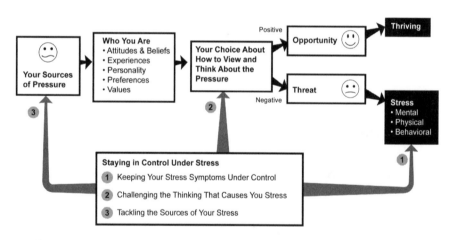

Figure 5.3 Staying in Control Under Stress

KEY TAKEAWAYS

- There are two sides to pressure: it can exhilarate and energize or it can drain and crush leaders.
- The negative response to pressure is stress.
- Stress is not always caused by major events; it can simply be the result of the daily grind and hassles.
- The key to controlling your stress to manageable proportions is to be aware of when you *are* stressed.
- Who you are as a person is a big factor in determining how you respond to pressure and the likelihood of becoming stressed.
- Negative thinking about situations and circumstances is likely to result in stress.
- You have a choice over how you think about things so that most stress is self-imposed.
- Symptoms of stress can be broken down into mental, physical, and behavioral categories.
- Be aware of subtle changes in your thoughts, bodily responses, and behavior to help you to recognize when you are stressed.
- There are three options open to you in dealing with stress: keeping your stress symptoms under control; challenging the thinking that causes you stress; tackling the sources of your stress.

Chapter 6

■ ■ ■

Keeping Your Stress Symptoms Under Control

KEY TOPICS

■ **Calming your mind**
■ **Controlling your physical symptoms**
■ **Adapting your behavior**

The underlying premise of this book is that being a *real* leader can be tough and even stressful. At times, it may cause you to lie awake at night worrying about how you are going to deliver difficult messages, or you may have doubts about your ability to deal with particularly tough situations. At other times, the seemingly overwhelming demands on your time may result in fatigue and even exhaustion. Those exercise sessions or relaxing time-outs that you find so helpful in enabling you to switch off may become fewer and fewer as your time becomes increasingly engulfed by an endless list of urgent to-dos.

Being able to keep your stress symptoms under control is important in enabling you to perform your role as a *real* leader effectively. This chapter describes strategies and tools that will help you achieve this. As you work through the pages that follow, try to keep an open mind. Some of the strategies and tools may seem a bit foreign, and you may feel they will take too much time and effort to master. This is not the case, and one of them could change your life, so stick with it!

Monitoring Your Stress

Marcy, a high-flying senior finance officer in the retail sector, told me she had "felt out of sorts" for a while but was unable to pinpoint exactly what the problem was and how to address it. Things came to a head when, as part of an annual 360-degree feedback process, she discovered a common theme among her direct reports and peers: she had become slower in making key decisions, was less accessible to her team, and had also become unpredictable in her moods. Marcy's desire to be a *real* leader again drove her to get to the root of the problem.

We began by focusing on days when she felt she was doing a good job as a leader, and compared them with those days she described as bad. I asked her to recall how she generally felt on those days. On bad days she referred to a number of different things, including sometimes feeling overwhelmed with the volume of work, having poor concentration, doubting herself, having little energy, feeling on edge, being hesitant to make decisions, feeling irritable, and also tending to overeat. She quickly recognized these were signs that she was stressed. On good days, Marcy felt pretty much at the opposite end of the continuum to these thoughts, feelings, and behaviors.

We constructed a set of continua with a midpoint for each, shown in Table 6.1, on the following page, to reflect each of the mental, physical, and behavioral factors that distinguished good days from bad days. Marcy used it on a daily basis to record where she was on each continuum. She also recorded her key work activities on each day.

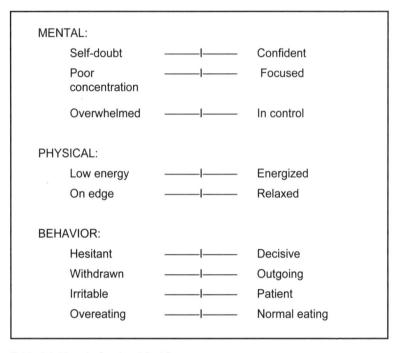

MENTAL:

    Self-doubt   ——I——   Confident

    Poor   ——I——   Focused
    concentration

    Overwhelmed   ——I——   In control

PHYSICAL:

    Low energy   ——I——   Energized

    On edge   ——I——   Relaxed

BEHAVIOR:

    Hesitant   ——I——   Decisive

    Withdrawn   ——I——   Outgoing

    Irritable   ——I——   Patient

    Overeating   ——I——   Normal eating

Table 6.1 Marcy's Good and Bad Days

This process achieved a number of outcomes that helped Marcy deal with her stress:

1. It enabled her to become much more aware of the pattern of her stress.

2. It helped her to recognize when she *was* stressed so that she could do something about it.

3. It enabled her to associate different symptoms with certain activities. For example, she generally felt overwhelmed when she began her day by going straight into a meeting, and she tended to be irritable when she had gone to

bed later than normal the previous night, usually after that extra glass of wine.

4. It formed the foundation of the plan we drew up for how Marcy would deal with her stress symptoms.

- **Self-doubt, poor concentration, overwhelmed:** She would tackle those tasks from her to-do list that were the most easily manageable and did not require much time. She also avoided scheduling meetings early in the morning so that she would have time to prepare for the day ahead.

- **Low energy:** When she experienced feelings of low energy she would go for a walk in the fresh air at lunchtime and listen to a playlist on her MP3 player that comprised music tracks she associated with high energy.

- **On edge:** I taught her a basic abdominal breathing technique (see later in this chapter) she would use when she felt on edge.

- **Hesitant:** She wrote a list of the key decisions she needed to make and made sure she made at least one each day.

- **Withdrawn:** In the past when Marcy felt withdrawn she had typically closed the door to her office. Her new plan was to leave it open when she felt this way. She also planned to do more "walkabouts" to pull her out of her withdrawn state.

- **Irritable:** The solution to this was simply to get to bed earlier and to save the wine left in the bottle for another evening.

- **Overeating:** Her plan when she was feeling under stress was to record everything she ate so that she was aware of the quantity of food she was consuming.

These are simple actions that helped Marcy enormously. I recommend that you go through the same process of working out the mental, physical, and behavioral effects stress has on you and then monitor them on a daily basis.

Meditative Relaxation Tools

Relaxation tools provide an effective way of helping you control your stress. Meditative relaxation has been around in one form or another for at least five thousand years. It has traditionally been associated with spiritual purposes, but its widespread use outside of any religious framework reflects the large number of people who use meditation as a mind-calming tool for personal growth and development. It is especially powerful in enabling leaders to control their mental stress symptoms. Meditation was popularized a number of years ago with the introduction of Transcendental Meditation to the West, which research[12] has shown to have numerous benefits, including:

- Reduced blood pressure

- Reduced concentration of lactic acid in the blood (associated with lower anxiety)

- Increased energy levels

- Heightened alertness

---

12. Herbert Benson, *Beyond the Relaxation Response*, Morrow, 1975.

• Reduced self-criticism

• Heightened self-esteem

Meditation typically involves concentrating on breathing and using a key word, known as a *mantra*, spoken silently on each exhalation. Focusing on the mantra helps to distract you from negative thoughts and serves as a means of clearing and calming your mind. This tool has proved very beneficial for both business leaders and athletes debilitated by stress. Typically, I have taught them two forms of relaxation: deep and quick.

1. The *deep* form of meditative relaxation, typically lasting between fifteen and twenty minutes, is generally practiced sitting or lying down, with your eyes shut. You then progress through various stages as follows:

   • Focusing on your breathing

   • Focusing on saying "one" silently to yourself on each breath out

   • Counting down from ten to one on each successive breath out

   • Focusing on saying "one" to yourself

   • Counting up from one to seven on each breath in

   • Opening your eyes

2. The *quick* form of meditative relaxation can be performed over a few seconds as a means of refocusing or calming your mind in those crucial moments just before and during an important situation. This simply involves focusing on

the mantra over three or four breaths out. Leaders I have worked with use this quick form of relaxation to compose themselves before announcing bad news or maybe to manage any anger, frustration, or other negative emotions when it is important to keep them under tight control.

Guidelines and scripts for the two forms of meditative relaxation are provided below.

Practicing Meditative Relaxation

Guidelines for practicing meditation are as follows:[13]

- Find a quiet environment where you will not be disturbed.

- Try not to meditate on a full stomach.

- Ideally, you should wear loose clothing, but if this is not feasible, then at least remove your shoes and loosen your belt if you notice any tightness around your waist.

- Find yourself a comfortable position. You will find it easier to meditate in the early stages if you lie on a sofa or bed. Do not cross your feet, arms, or legs.

- It may help if you place your hands on your stomach to enable you to feel the steady rhythm of your breaths in and out.

- You may experience feeling heavy or perhaps a light,

---

13. Meditation can release emotions that cause problems for people with a history of mental illness. In these circumstances, medical advice should be sought before practicing meditative relaxation.

floating sensation. These are normal experiences. If you experience anything that is remotely unpleasant, stop meditating.

- If you are distracted by any noises or thoughts, do not try to ignore them. Instead, let them pass and gently return to your intended focus.

- Approach meditation with a nonjudgmental, passive attitude. If you think it will not work, then it will not work!

- Try to meditate every day. You will get better as you practice it.

- Meditation is often easier if you keep your eyes closed.

Deep Relaxation

Set aside at least fifteen minutes for the session. It might be helpful in the early stages if you make a recording to guide you through the meditation process. Follow the process below.

Make yourself comfortable.
(Thirty-second interval)

Close your eyes and focus on your breathing.
(Continue for one minute)

Now focus on saying "one" to yourself as you breathe out.
(Continue for five minutes)

Now focus on counting down from ten to one on successive breaths out until you reach one, and continue with one.
(When you reach one continue for five minutes)

*Now focus on counting up from one to seven on succes-
sive breaths in. Take deeper breaths as you count up.*

On seven open your eyes.

Quick Relaxation

This form of relaxation can be practiced in most situations, but
obviously not when it might put you in danger (e.g., when driving
a car). Follow the process below.

Close your eyes or focus on a small, static object.

Focus on saying "one" to yourself on each breath out.

Continue for three or four breaths.

Open your eyes, or stop focusing on the small object.

Experiment with these two forms and see if they work for you.
Quick relaxation, in particular, could be of benefit when you need
to calm down quickly. Remember that relaxation in this form is a
skill, so you need to practice it.

Imagery

Imagery is a powerful tool that can be used for several purposes when it comes to gaining control over the mind and body.
When used for controlling stress symptoms, imagery acts as
a means of distracting you from your symptoms and focusing
you instead on thoughts that help to calm your mind and, sub-

sequently, your body. Once you have decided on an image of something or somewhere you find very relaxing, focusing on it for a few minutes or even seconds will help to compose you when needed.

The image you use is completely your choice. It might be a quiet beach, beautiful countryside, mountains, soaking in a warm bath, sitting by a cozy fire, etc. The key is to visualize and feel yourself in the scene in as much detail as possible so that you become absorbed in it. This will help to reduce any tension you are experiencing. You might want to record a script of the relaxing scene and then use it to guide yourself through it. A sample imagery scene is provided below.

Imagery Script

You are strolling along a beautiful, deserted white sand beach. You are barefoot and can feel the soft and warm sand beneath your feet and between your toes as you walk along the water's edge. You can hear the sound of the surf as the waves ebb and flow. The sound is hypnotic, relaxing you more and more. The water is a beautiful greeny-blue flecked with whitecaps far out where the waves are cresting. The sound of the waves breaking on the shore lulls you deeper and deeper into relaxation. You draw in the fresh, salty smell of the air with each breath. Your skin glows with the warmth of the sun. You can feel a gentle breeze against your cheek and ruffling your hair. Take in the whole scene as you feel very calm and at ease.

An important aspect of the above script is that it uses language that appeals to the senses of sight, touch, hearing, and smell.

Multisensory words increase the power of the image so you can experience it as if you were actually there, thus making it conducive to relaxation.

Why not design your own image? Describe it in vivid detail and make sure it appeals to as many different senses as possible. What does it look like? Are there any sounds? What is the temperature? What are you in physical contact with? What does the air smell like? What colors are prominent? As with meditative relaxation, remember to practice imagery. If you can create an image that works for you, you will find it more relaxing as you continue to use it.

Abdominal Breathing

Abdominal breathing is an effective tool for dealing with the physical symptoms of stress. Your breathing is a good indicator of the level of tension in your body. As tension increases, your breathing usually becomes shallower and more rapid, involving the upper chest area only. When you are relaxed, you breathe more fully and deeply from your abdomen. Learning to breathe in this way alleviates the physical symptoms of stress, and even helps you to relax once you become good at it. Here is a sample script that shows you how to breathe from the abdomen.

Abdominal Breathing Exercise

Place one hand on your abdomen just below your rib cage.

Inhale slowly and deeply through your nose into the bottom of your lungs. Your hand should actually rise and your chest should move only slightly while your abdomen expands.

When you have taken in a full breath, pause for a moment and then exhale slowly through your nose or mouth. As you exhale, allow your whole body to just "let go."

Do ten slow, full abdominal breaths. Keep your breathing smooth and regular. It will help if you count to four on the inhalation and then count to four again on the exhalation.

Remember to pause at the end of each inhalation before breathing out.

Practice the abdominal breathing exercise above for five minutes every day for a couple of weeks. You will improve as you practice and find it very beneficial in helping you to reduce any physical tension you experience when under stress.

Adapting Your Behavior

People around you will not know about your mental and physical stress symptoms because only you know what is happening to you. It is only the third and final category of stress symptoms, behavioral, that are observable to others. As a *real* leader, your people will be watching you very carefully, so you will need to be alert to when your stress is impacting on your behavior with them. Developing self-awareness and recognizing how your behavior changes when you are stressed therefore assumes even greater significance. Below are some examples of behavioral changes typical of leaders under stress:

- Poor prioritizing

- Micromanaging

- Short-term focus

- Less time spent coaching

- Placing excessive expectations on those around them

- Inconsistent moods

- Poor listening

- Indecisiveness

- Showing less care and concern for others around them

- Working long hours

- Impatience

- Intolerance

- And many more too numerous to mention here

Do you recognize any of them in yourself? Why not get feedback on changes in your behavior when you are stressed from people who work with you and know you pretty well? Become more aware of specific changes in your behavior when you are stressed and the impact it has on those around you. Then work on doing something about them!

And Do Not Forget to Work on Your Lifestyle!

Being a *real* leader can be a fulfilling and stimulating experience. But, as I highlighted in Master Class 1, at times the pressures and expectations on you can be enormous and reach the point where they spill over into your life outside the workplace. I have already described how achieving a good work-life balance can be a major challenge, and this becomes even harder when you experience stress. In fact, the life you lead can become unhealthy if you are not careful.

Your reflections on the questions below will give you an indication of how healthy, or not, your lifestyle currently is. Do you:

- get sufficient good quality sleep?

- exercise regularly?

- make time for rest during the week?

- follow a healthy diet?

- take vacations?

- make time to socialize with your friends?

- devote time to things you find relaxing, such as reading, listening to music, etc.?

- spend enough quality time with your loved ones?

- drink a volume of alcohol that is within health guidelines?

- moderate your caffeine intake?

These health indicators become even more important when you are stressed. But what typically happens when people are stressed is that they do things that exacerbate it: they drink too much alcohol and caffeine, they eat unhealthy convenience foods more frequently, they stop exercising, they go to bed later than usual, and so it goes on.

Yet again, self-awareness is the starting point. Make yourself aware of how stress affects your lifestyle, and then do something about it. It is not difficult. For example, if you drink an excessive amount of caffeine-laced coffee during periods of stress and this increases your sleeping problem, there is a pretty easy solution to this particular symptom!

So What Will You Do?

Whether you like it or not, there will be times when your *real* leadership role causes you stress, and you will need strategies and tools to help you control your stress symptoms. Devote time and effort to experimenting with the tools described in this chapter. To set yourself off in the right direction, spend a few minutes working through Time-Out 6.

TIME-OUT 6

CHOOSE SOMETHING THAT WILL WORK FOR YOU

You now know about a variety of tools and strategies for dealing with your stress symptoms. Remind yourself of the symptoms you typically experience when you are stressed and then think about how the tools and strategies described in this chapter will help you control those symptoms. Choose one or two that appeal to you and think about how you will use them in specific situations.

When you have found something that works for you, practice and perfect it; it will prove invaluable in those moments when the stress of your *real* leadership role threatens to overpower you and you need to regain your composure.

KEY TAKEAWAYS

- Recognizing the symptoms you experience when you are stressed and being aware of when you are experiencing them is the key to being able to control them.
- Learn to associate different stress symptoms with certain activities.
- Meditative relaxation is a powerful tool for calming the mind.
- Imaging relaxing scenes is a powerful tool for calming your mind and body.
- Abdominal breathing is an effective way of reducing the tension in your body.
- You may need to adapt your behaviors when under stress.
- Leading a healthy lifestyle will help you better manage stress.

Chapter 7

■ ■ ■

Challenging the Thinking
That Causes You Stress

KEY TOPICS

- ■ Blocking out negative thoughts
- ■ Reframing negative thinking
- ■ Seeking others' views and perspectives

The responsibilities and accountabilities that go with the role of being a *real* leader require you to remain calm and rational at all times. As a *real* leader, you are the person who will be looked to for reassurance when your people are catastrophizing in the midst of the toughest economic times. You will find yourself in the front line of restructures, mergers, and acquisitions where uncertainty and anxiety are rife; they may even threaten your own job security. And what about those people who you just know are out there thinking they can do your job better than you?

In the sorts of circumstances described above, it would be easy to get caught in a downward spiral of negative thinking that inevitably results in stress. I will refer to this type of thinking as "stinking thinking" because of its potential debilitating, nasty consequences. This chapter describes ways in which you can recognize your negative thinking patterns and gain control over them.

Do You Engage in Stinking Thinking?

Changing stinking thinking into positive thinking is not easy. It can be a major challenge for leaders whose personalities, previous experiences, and/or attitudes and beliefs mean they have natural tendencies to look on the dark side. If *you* engage in stinking thinking, the first step in dealing with it is to realize and remind yourself that you have a *choice* about the way you think, and that you can actually alter your mode of thinking. Once again, self-awareness will underpin any change you wish to make. Have a look through the typical stinking thought patterns below and note those you engage in when under pressure.

- "The world's coming to an end" thinking is about catastrophizing in the form of blowing things out of proportion and thinking the worst may, will, or has happened: "I'm not properly prepared for my big presentation tomorrow—it will be a disaster."

- "They're all the same" thinking involves overgeneralizing by applying your own thoughts, feelings, and attitudes across all people and situations: "These guys always try to catch me out by asking awkward questions during my presentation."

- "Second-guessing" thinking is making assumptions about what others are thinking and with negative repercussions for yourself: "The audience looks bored. They're not interested in what I'm saying."

- "Yes, but" thinking reflects taking positive events and twisting them into negative ones: "Okay, so everyone told me my presentation was good, but nobody said it was great."

- "It can't be done" thinking involves looking into the future and predicting a negative outcome: "I'll never be able to keep this audience engaged for a whole hour."

- "It has to be perfect" thinking means any small misstep will be viewed as a failure: "This presentation has to be perfect."

- "Should and must" thinking is where you constantly remind yourself of what you *should* or *must* do: "I must make a good impression in the presentation."

The thought patterns described above are by no means exhaustive, and I am sure you will have your own particular way of stinking thinking. However, I am also sure that you engage in at least one of the thought patterns above, because most leaders do! Thoughts like these need to be addressed because they only serve to exacerbate the stress you experience. Spend a few minutes working through Time-Out 7.1 below to identify any stinking thought patterns *you* engage in.

TIME-OUT 7.1

DO YOU ENGAGE IN STINKING THINKING?

Do you engage in any of the following stinking thought patterns? "The world's coming to an end," "They're all the same," "Second-guessing," "Yes, but," "It can't be done," "It has to be perfect," "Should and must."

So what can you do about your stinking thinking? Fortunately, there are several ways of changing or at least modifying your thinking that will enable you to control stress to manageable levels in high-pressure situations. These are described in the following sections.

Blocking Out Automatic Negative Thoughts

Stress symptoms often include what are termed "automatic negative thoughts." These are the thoughts that just seem to jump into your head when you are in that vicious stress cycle: "I'm stupid," "I've lost control," "I'm not good enough for this role," and so on. Left unaddressed, such thoughts will rapidly consume you and drag you down into an even deeper level of stress.

I coached Martin, a senior leader in a financial institution who was particularly affected by automatic negative thoughts. He referred to "being paralyzed" by thoughts about how inadequate he was as a leader when he learned from his team about poor monthly revenue numbers. He was unable to control these thoughts, and they rapidly turned into even worse ones in which he convinced himself that he was about to lose his job. He became transfixed by these thoughts at a time when he needed to be thinking clearly and flexibly.

I provided Martin with a number of ideas and tools for combating automatic negative thoughts; these are described below with the intention of stimulating your own ideas around what might be most appropriate for you.

Thought-Stopping Statements

The problem with automatic negative thoughts is that once they infiltrate your conscious mind, they can multiply and spread very quickly. The vicious cycle that automatic negative thoughts drag you into can be broken by thought-stopping statements, the simplest of which is just telling yourself to "stop." Martin liked this one because of its simplicity and we enhanced this tool by including an image of a red stop sign. Other thought-stopping statements that might be effective for you include "Don't go there," "Take control," "Wait a minute." Experiment with a few different statements and find one that works for you.

Catching ANTS

Another simple tool for dealing with automatic negative thoughts is based on their acronym, ANTS. The key to this tool is to recognize and imagine that you have ANTS busily building nests in your head that need to be caught and disposed of. Again, experiment with different statements about ants or conjure up an image of dealing with ants to stop them in their tracks. Martin used this tool as an alternative to the red stop sign. He found that simply thinking "ANTS" was sufficient to stop them when he had practiced it enough.

Positive Imagery

Negative thoughts are not always in the form of self-statements and often fly into your head as images of failure. For example, Martin sometimes had images flash through his mind of him messing up the introduction to a presentation he was about to deliver. He learned not to start the presentation before he had blocked out these images and imagined himself, instead, beginning the presentation really well. Positive imagery is a very powerful tool in these types of circumstances. Try to recall the following statement as a stimulus for blocking out negative images:

"If you think you will perform well you often will; if you think you will perform badly you always will!"

Reframing Your Stinking Thinking

I delivered a presentation, "Leading in Tough Times," to the top one hundred leaders of a large manufacturing company as the seriousness of the economic difficulties was becoming very apparent during the latter part of 2008. These leaders knew they were in for a rocky ride, and the organization was doing its best to prepare them. I was struck by the CEO's opening remarks in providing the context for the session. I have paraphrased below the key messages he shared:

"There is no hiding from the fact that tough times are here, and they are with us for the next eighteen months at the very least. Now, there are two ways that we can look at this as leaders of this organization. We can view the glass as half empty, but we can also view the glass as half full. There will be times when the glass definitely is half empty, and we must not shy away from doing what needs to be done during those times. But there will also be times when the glass is half full and there will be opportunities for our business. We must ensure that we are not so consumed by the glass-half-empty mindset that we fail to recognize and seize those opportunities. One thing is for sure in these times of uncertainty: the good times will return and when they do we will emerge stronger. These tough times provide us all with a fantastic opportunity to learn and develop as leaders."

Here was a classic case of reframing thinking about what most of the leaders in the audience were probably dreading.

Sometimes, it just is not possible to change the situations that cause stress, but you can change your emotional response using reframing tools that enable you to control how you interpret, explain, and judge the situations you encounter. Reframing your thoughts involves recognizing, challenging, and changing negative, distorted thinking that causes stress into thoughts that are rational and allow you to see the situation through a different lens that provides you with a calmer, beneficial perspective. It enables you to examine your negative thoughts "under a microscope" and check how rational and valid these interpretations are. Some tools for reframing your stinking thinking are described below.

Using Questions to Reframe Your Stinking Thinking

Learn to ask yourself some questions when you are in pressure situations and you become aware of stinking thinking. I am sure that you will be able to identify your own questions for maximum impact, but a few possible ones are listed below:

- Is there another way to view this situation?

- Is there anything positive I can take from this situation?

- Have I got all the information?

- If I had a month to live, how important would this be?

- What is the worst thing that could happen?

A major problem with stinking thinking is that it too easily becomes fact. Questions like those above will help you see your thinking not as fact but rather as the way you are viewing your world right now. They will help you to see the inaccuracies and distortions in your thinking so that you are able to replace them with more realistic and accurate thoughts.

Taking Ownership of Your Thoughts

When stinking thinking leads to stress, you often create a "choice-less" reality in your mind. In other words, you forget you are in control of your thoughts and that you have a choice about thinking this way or not. An internal monologue that includes thoughts like "I have to," "I must," "I should," and "I can't" forces you into a downward spiral difficult to emerge from. Try changing your "I have to" and "I can't" thoughts to "I choose to" and "I choose not to" thoughts respectively. This will help you take ownership of your thoughts and exercise the choices you have probably forgotten you have.

Seeing It from the Outside

This tool is really simple. When you find yourself in the grips of stinking thinking, reflect on what you would say to a close friend who informed you that he or she was experiencing those same thoughts. Give yourself the same rational, encouraging support you would give your friend. This will enable you to put your stinking thinking into perspective.

For example, imagine you received an e-mail from your boss at the end of a week in which your team had reported worse than promised quarterly figures. The e-mail requests your presence in his office at 8:00 Monday morning. Instead of worrying all week-end about the prospect of having to defend your actions—or being given a stern lecture or perhaps even being let go—imagine your-self sitting down with a friend who tells you that he is in exactly the same situation and with exactly the same thoughts racing through his mind. Imagine what you would say to him. Think of all the reasons his boss might want to see your friend. Perhaps it is because his boss wants to talk to him about an exciting new opportunity. Perhaps his boss wants to get your friend's views on an important decision he is mulling over. Perhaps it *is* about the figures and his boss wants to understand how he can support your friend. This will help *you* to stay rational and enjoy your weekend.

Real Leaders Ask for Support

It will be abundantly clear by now that stress is often caused by thought patterns that are both negative and irrational. The previous section described how reframing your thoughts is a powerful tool for alleviating stress. However, that can be difficult to do on your own when you are so entrenched in your own point of view. Such circumstances often call for the input of respected and trusted individuals who can support you in developing other ways of viewing the world. Indeed, our research on mental toughness highlights "seeking support when you need it" as a key attribute.

This does not always translate so easily into the business world, where people may be afraid to ask for support in fear that it is viewed as a sign of weakness. "I have to know all the answers" is a phrase I have heard too often among leaders. This is bound to cause stress when you find yourself not knowing the answer to a question or challenge posed by your team. Getting someone else's perspective who can provide a rationale on why it is unrealistic to know everything will help you to challenge your own point of view.

Think carefully about who you select. You will derive little benefit from confiding in people who engage in similar stinking thinking to yourself. Nor do you need people telling you how and what to think. The best sources of support will be people who ask you questions like "On what evidence are your thoughts based?" and "What are the other ways you might think about this?" This will not only force you to think about the validity of your thoughts, but will also get you into the habit of asking yourself similar questions in the future.

Using this tool effectively will require you to view asking for help as a strength rather than a weakness. This is what *safe* leaders do not do because they perceive it to be too risky to admit to colleagues that they need help. As a *real* leader, however, you should be willing and able to disclose enough of yourself to admit that you do not have all the answers and invite your team's contribution.

So What Will You Do?

As a *real* leader you will know about the need to present a composed and rational exterior to your people and key stakeholders at all times. But, like everyone else, you are a human being with the same frailties and sensitivities, and your inner self may not always match the calmness you portray. Sometimes you will have the same uncertainties and anxieties you are trying to quell among your people; you are by no means exempt from the propensity for stinking thinking! Spend some time working through Time-Out 7.2 as a means of enhancing how you will challenge the thinking that causes you stress in the future.

Strategies and tools for challenging the thinking that causes you stress are more effective in the longer term than those that focus on symptoms. Experiment with and practice the one(s) you have identified above. It could make an enormous difference to how you deal with pressure and stress.

TIME-OUT 7.2

CHALLENGING THE THINKING THAT CAUSES YOU STRESS

This chapter has covered the following strategies for dealing with stinking thinking:

- Blocking out negative thoughts
- Reframing stinking thinking
- Asking for support

Which of these strategies, or elements of different ones, most appeals to you? In what situations will it or they be most useful? How do you intend to put it or them into practice?

KEY TAKEAWAYS

- ■ Learn to recognize when you are engaging in stinking thinking.
- ■ Identify your typical automatic negative thoughts (ANTS) and learn to block them out.
- ■ Learn to reframe the stinking thinking that causes you stress.
- ■ Seek support from respected and trusted others to challenge the way you think about situations that cause you stress.

Chapter 8

■ ■ ■

Tackling the Sources of Your Stress

KEY TOPICS

■ **Making things happen**
■ **Creating choices that take the stress out of situations**
■ **Maximizing supports, minimizing constraints**

Real leaders are fully aware of the need to address the source of the pressure that triggers the stinking thinking that leads to stress. They also know this is often the most difficult of the coping tools to implement. This, together with the too frequent assumption and acceptance that little can be done to alleviate the pressure, means that some leaders never even consider this strategy until things get so serious that there is no alternative. This is another key difference between *safe* and *real* leaders: *real* leaders tackle issues head-on while *safe* leaders typically avoid them.

Making Things Happen

Real leaders tackle stress head-on by making something happen to change the situation and circumstances that are at the source. They do this via two strategies and tools:

1. **Challenging assumptions.** Stress sources are often ignored or avoided by *safe* leaders, who focus instead on dealing with their symptoms and stinking thinking. This is because they typically assume they have no control or influence over the source and so do not waste valuable time and effort in challenging "the system." For *safe* leaders, this may be too much of a risk anyway. As a *real* leader, the starting point for you is actually to challenge your assumptions before you are in a position to challenge the system. Do not assume, for example, that unrealistic performance targets are not negotiable—indeed, the assumption of the goal-setter may be that they must be realistic because you have not challenged them!

2. **Making decisions.** A further difference between *real* and *safe* leaders lies in the whole area of decision making; *real* leaders are more ready and willing to make important decisions, whether it be the tough ones that may impact detrimentally on some of their people or the personal decisions that impact only on themselves. But even for *real* leaders this becomes more difficult under stress. This can make things worse because dealing with stress often requires you to make decisions that will enable you to cope with it more effectively. For example, work overload spanning over a prolonged period has the potential to leave you burned out if you do not tackle it. Deciding how important being successful in your career is to you, and then deciding how you will balance your time and efforts to achieve these aspirations against the other demands in your life, cannot be delayed if you are to deal with this source of stress effectively. Similarly, deciding how you will approach upcoming change rather than being a passive *safe* leader, and sometimes "victim," can radically alter your experience of change. And if you are regularly missing out on selection for those more senior positions you aspire to, you have a

decision to make about whether to move on or stick it out. Delaying such decisions merely prolongs the stress and the need to withstand its symptoms.

Making things happen is an important step in becoming a *real* leader. Sometimes, challenging assumptions and making decisions are closely linked. A couple of years ago, I was asked to coach David, whose boss was the global head of the IT function of a large utilities company. David was the head of a large regional team and had a reputation for sitting on the fence and not making the decisions his boss needed from him. It soon became apparent in my one-on-ones with David that he had plenty of ideas about how things could be different and better in the IT function. But he had never actually voiced any of them because he believed his boss's micromanagement of him reflected a leader who was closed to new ways of doing things.

David was stressed by the situation. He felt powerless, stifled, and frustrated that he had so little influence in such a senior leader position. The key to David's stress was his untested assumption that his boss was micromanaging him because his boss was a "control freak." What also emerged during our conversations was that David suspected his boss did not value or trust his direct report's judgment.

The solution was quite simple. Since his assumptions remained unchallenged, he had to find some way of testing them. Before doing so, David reached the decision that if his assumptions were valid, he would move on to another job. He then wrote a proposal for the restructure of the IT function in his region and sent it to his boss. Within forty-eight hours, his boss phoned David to tell him how much he had enjoyed reading the proposal, that he thought many of the ideas should be implemented across the global function, and that this is what he knew David had been capable of all along.

David's stress had been caused by stinking thinking that he had no influence and that his boss did not respect his ability. Making things happen turned the situation, and David's stress, on its head. It is a shame it had not happened sooner!

Creating Choices That Change Situations

My thinking about this strategy for addressing stress sources originated from my work with elite athletes. The world's best athletes do not achieve that status without incredible commitment, dedication, and hard work. They will be training when you and I are tucked up in our warm beds on cold winter mornings. They will be tucked up in their beds when you and I are enjoying a beer or glass of wine at our friend's party. When they dine out, they will eat only those foods their nutrition advisors have prescribed, while we will feast on anything that takes our fancy. When these athletes are asked at the end of their careers if all the sacrifices they made were worth it, I have witnessed virtually all of them say, "I didn't make any sacrifices, I made choices."

Numerous senior leaders have told me about the "sacrifices" they have to make because of their demanding roles and how they contribute to their stress: spending less time at home, always on a plane, never enough time. Those who thrive in these circumstances have a completely different mindset: they *choose* to do these things. And they make sure that the time they do have to devote to other things is of the highest quality, because they are making a *choice* rather than meeting an *obligation*. This type of mindset is crucial in helping *real* leaders thrive under the spotlight. It also helps them achieve a work-life balance they have chosen as opposed to being a "victim" of circumstance.

A high-flying lawyer I coached, Doug, was enjoying his success but was conscious that his rising profile within the firm meant he spent less and less time at home. His ever-increasing workload, together with his long commute into the office, meant he seldom saw his young children before they were tucked up in bed each night. Weekends were the only time Doug saw them awake, but he was so fatigued that he did not have the energy to devote much more than a passing interest in them. His hitherto very understanding wife was becoming less understanding, and the marriage was showing a few cracks. It became evident that Doug was viewing the lack of time with his family as a sacrifice that just had to be made to achieve success. But it was also evident that an intense guilt was gnawing away at him. The situation was causing him enormous stress.

I suggested that Doug view his situation in the context of the framework shown in Figure 8.1. This is how I have come to think about the work-life balance issue that faces the vast majority of senior leaders. The horizontal axis distinguishes between "choice," what people have the freedom to choose to do, and "obligation," what they feel compelled to do. The vertical axis distinguishes between "at work" and "outside work" activities.

Using this framework, Doug was able to see how he had viewed working long hours as an obligation, or something he felt compelled to do, since he associated it with being recognized and successful. He also realized how he thought he "must" spend time with his family; it was an obligation of being a father and husband. In essence, he was trying to deal with two competing obligations so that a sacrifice was inevitable. The solution was actually quite simple. Doug had to adopt a different mindset and shift both "working long hours" and "spending time with family" into the relevant "choice" quadrants. Since both became choices, making a sacrifice was taken out of the equation. He chose to spend more time with his family and less time at work. In addition, because both were no longer obligations, he saw each in a

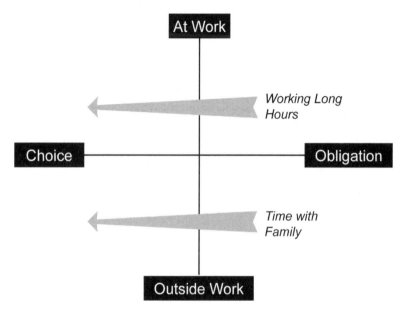

Figure 8.1 Changing Obligations into Choices

more positive light, which helped to enhance the quality of how he spent his time both at work and at home.

Do *you* make sacrifices? Do you feel you are missing out on other things in life you would prefer to be doing because your leadership role requires so much of your time? Do you feel guilty because you are with your loved ones less than you and they would like? You have options around how you can view the decisions you have made, because that is what they are: decisions. You have decided on the job and role you fill; you have decided to work the hours you do. So they are only obligations if that is how you view them. Why not consider them as choices you have made? It will make a real difference to how you view your existence and help you to tackle the situations that cause you stress.

Minimizing Your Constraints *and* Maximizing Your Supports

A classic response to stress is to focus on the negative elements of the demands on you. These are often in the form of constraints that frustrate you or perhaps leave you feeling helpless. This classic response also involves forgetting about the things that are there to support you. An important aspect of *real* leadership is to gain as much control as possible over, or minimize, constraints *and* to use supports to their maximum effect.

The exercise below will take you through a process where you will identify the demands on you in your leader role, the constraints that get in the way of satisfying those demands, and the supports you have at your disposal. I have used this exercise with numerous leaders, and it has had a major impact on helping them deal with stress in every case.

Demands, Supports, and Constraints Exercise

- Think about your role and identify and list the *demands* on you. The list should include everything that you do and is expected of you. Try to be specific rather than coming up with a small number of general demands.

- Now think about and list the *supports* you have at your disposal to help satisfy the demands you have identified. Do not try to generate supports for each specific demand; instead, view the demands you have listed as a whole "package."

- Move on to identify the *constraints* that currently limit you and perhaps get in the way of satisfying the demands. Note that a support can also be a constraint. Again, do not try to generate constraints for each specific demand; instead, view the demands you have listed as a whole "package."

- Look back over your lists of demands, supports, and constraints and add any you may have missed.

- Now focus on your list of *supports* and work out how much support you actually get from each. Using a scale from 1 ("I get no support at all") to 10 ("I get total support"), rate how much support you currently derive from each one you have listed.

- Now focus on your list of *constraints*, and using a scale from 1 ("I have no influence or control") to 10 ("I have total influence or control"), rate how much influence or control you have over each constraint.

- Have a close look at your ratings for the two lists. Are there any themes, or "aha" moments? Have you rated all of your supports as 10s? Have you rated all of your constraints as 1s? If not (and I have never encountered a single leader who has), then you have some work to do! You are not controlling constraints that you have some control over, and you are not getting optimum support from those at your disposal. Essentially, you are failing to minimize your constraints and maximize your supports.

A Case Study

Before proceeding to the next step, I want to tell you about a leader who has benefited from this exercise. Michelle, in her early forties, is a board director of a large public relations company. She completed the same exercise you have just worked through, and the output is shown below.

Michelle's Demands, Supports, and Constraints

Demands

- Hit growth target

- Hit profit target

- Come up with strategy and plan

- Communicate the strategy and plan

- Challenge people to raise the bar

- Report to the MD

- Work with fellow directors

- Lead my team

- Be visible to my people

- Inspire my people

- Make tough decisions

- Make the right decisions

- Mother to two young children

- Get a good work-life balance

Supports (Rating)

- Direct reports (7)

- Other directors (5)

- Personal assistant (5)

- My experience and skills (8)

- E-mail (8)

- Laptop computer (8)

- MD (7)

- Performance development reviews (5)

- Budget (5)

- Partner (9)

Constraints (Rating)

- Direct reports—don't take initiative (7)

- Other directors—silo mentality and behaviors (4)

- E-mail—too many (4)

- Slow market (1)

- Shareholder expectations—too unrealistic (1)

- Lack of time (4)

- Some direct reports—lack of appropriate experience (4)

- New IT system (2)

- MD (3)

- Open plan working—too much noise (3)

- Too much travel—tiring (4)

- Having to get home early to see my kids (4)

Through this exercise, Michelle realized that many of the frustrations she experienced in her role were caused by things she had control over but had not been addressing. We used the output of the exercise as a means of developing a plan to deal with the sources of pressure and potential stress. As the first step toward minimizing all her constraints and maximizing all her supports, I asked Michelle to select a maximum of one constraint she had not rated as a 1, and one support she had not rated as a 10. The following criteria were used to guide her selection:

1. It was in her control to change something about them.

2. It was realistic that something could be changed about them.

3. If she changed something about them it would make a *real* impact, rather than merely "papering over the cracks."

4. Any changes she made would start to have an impact in a relatively short time frame.

Michelle selected "personal assistant" as the support she wanted to work on and "other directors—silo mentality and behaviors" as the constraint she wanted to address. Together, we identified specific actions that involved talking to her personal assistant about the support she needed but was not getting, and about stimulating discussions at board meetings around adopting a more unified approach and mindset to running the company. When she had made significant progress toward her desired outcomes, Michelle moved on to minimizing other constraints and maximizing other supports that would make a real difference to her effectiveness in her role.

Identifying demands, supports, and constraints is a simple and effective way of developing a strategy for dealing with the sources of stress. It helps leaders who have previously lost sight of how much control and influence they have over what happens around them. Michelle had "learned" to accept that she could do nothing about her personal assistant's lack of support and her fellow directors' silo mentality. This exercise enabled her to recognize that she did have some control, and her actions resulted in a significant reduction of her stress.

Your Demands, Supports, and Constraints Action Plan

- Return to the demands, supports, and constraints you identified earlier and remind yourself what they are.

- Focus on the *supports* that you did not rate as a 10 in terms of the level of support you currently receive. Using the criteria below, choose one or two that you would like to work on:

  1. It should be in your control to do something about it.

  2. The changes you wish to make should be realistic.

  3. Any changes you make will have a real impact, rather than merely "papering over the cracks."

  4. Any changes will start to have an impact in a relatively short time frame.

- List the supports to work on and record any actions you intend to take.

- Now focus on the *constraints* you did not rate as a 1 in terms of the level of control or influence you have. Using the same criteria you applied to your supports, select one or two constraints you would like to work on.

- List the constraints and record any actions you intend to take.

Like any action plan, it will only be as good as what you do with it. It is up to you to make things happen in order to maximize your supports and minimize your constraints. It could make a big difference!

So What Will You Do?

As a *real* leader you are in a strong position to tackle the situations and circumstances that cause you stress. You are the one who can control and influence many of the factors in the environment that contribute to your stress. So what will you do?

Spend a few minutes working through Time-Out 8.

TIME-OUT 8

TACKLING THE SOURCES OF YOUR STRESS

This chapter has covered the following strategies for tackling the sources of your stress:

---

continued

- Making things happen
- Creating choices that change situations
- Maximizing supports and minimizing constraints

Which of these strategies and tools, or elements of different ones, most appeals to you? How do you intend to put it or them into practice?

Important in enabling you to tackle the sources of your stress successfully will be your drive and determination to address them head-on and to make things happen. Work out what you can control and control it!

KEY TAKEAWAYS

- ■ Tackle the things that cause you stress head-on.
- ■ Challenge your assumptions about what is possible.
- ■ Seize the initiative and make things happen.
- ■ Change situations and circumstances by making choices.
- ■ Maximize your supports and minimize your constraints.

That Concludes Master Class 2

This is the conclusion of Master Class 2, and you should now be in the position where you have decided on some tools and strategies for staying in control under the inevitable stress that comes with being a *real* leader. You will be better able to control your stress symptoms and to challenge and change the stinking thinking that causes your stress. But always remember that the most effective strategy is to tackle the situations and circumstances that are the sources of your stress.

Master Class 3

■■■

Strengthening Your Self-Belief in Your Ability as a *Real* Leader

OBJECTIVES

■ To enlighten you on what self-belief is

■ To guide you in developing and enhancing your self-esteem as a *real* leader

■ To equip you with strategies and tools for building your self-confidence to meet the many different demands of being a *real* leader

■■■

Chapter 9

■ ■ ■

What Is Self-Belief?

KEY TOPICS

■ The importance of self-belief for *real* leaders
■ The difference between self-belief, self-esteem, and self-confidence
■ The relationship that exists between self-esteem and self-confidence

I have never failed to be astounded by the impact self-belief has on people's lives. I first discovered its power in my work with elite athletes. In a world where there is virtually nothing to choose between the top few in any sport, self-belief, and being able to maintain it under pressure, is the critical differentiator. The same is true in the business world where it is an essential part of the makeup of *real* leaders. It is much easier to thrive on pressure when you believe in yourself.

Unfortunately, self-belief can be fragile, particularly in leaders in highly visible positions. As a *real* leader, you need robust and resilient self-belief if you are to be open to challenges and new ideas, to make those difficult and sometimes unpopular decisions, to challenge orthodoxy, and to put yourself in the firing line during tough times. And if you are to succeed in creating an environment where high performance is inevitable and sustainable, then demonstrating belief in your people and their ability to achieve the vision is also crucial.

This master class explores what self-belief is and describes strategies and tools that will help you develop and strengthen your own self-belief so that it remains robust and resilient under the pressure of being a *real* leader.

The Power of Self-Belief

I know you will have heard or read about the following story on numerous occasions, but I will remind you of it anyway because it epitomizes the power of self-belief. In 1954, the goal of running a sub-four-minute mile, which had been around since Victorian times, was believed to be insurmountable. It was argued that a human being was incapable of covering a mile in less than four minutes because its oxygen-carrying capacity was simply inadequate to the task. Australian John Landy, who had been pursuing the sub-four-minute dream and had gotten tantalizingly close on a number of occasions, finally admitted defeat, stating that he agreed it just was not possible. British runner Roger Bannister, who had been quietly plotting his own means of breaking through the barrier, refused to be swayed by such self-defeating talk. Soon after Landy's public submission, on a windy and rain-soaked day in Oxford in May 1954, Bannister ran the mile in 3 minutes 59.4 seconds. Amazingly, Landy ran 3 minutes 57.9 seconds 46 days later, bettering Bannister's time by 1.5 seconds. There were sixteen sub-four minute-milers by 1956.

There are actually two stories in one here about the power of belief. The first is one about how lack of belief constrained Landy for so long from achieving what he was really capable of. But look at what happened when he was shown that the sub-four-minute mile *was* possible; he not only broke through the barrier himself, he smashed through it. The second is about Bannister's long-standing belief that four minutes could be bettered. It drove him to plan how he could achieve it, knowing that he *would*.

Bannister's mentality, which enabled him to achieve what was seemingly "impossible" to others, is probably best understood in the philosophy he espoused on the fiftieth anniversary of the first sub-four-minute mile in 2004:

> However ordinary each of us may seem, we are all in some way special and can do things that are extraordinary, perhaps until then even thought impossible.[14]

This is the mindset that enabled him to believe that what athletes had talked and dreamt about for many years, and which other athletes believed beyond their reach, was within his capability. Bannister was certain he could break the four-minute barrier because he knew it was not a physical barrier that stood in the way, but a mental one.

Of course, self-belief drives destiny and whether people succeed or fail in achieving their dreams in all spheres of life. The importance of belief in the commercial world was recognized long ago by Henry Ford, founder of the Ford Motor Company, who said, "If you think you can, you're right. If you think you can't, you're right." The obstacle to achieving the "impossible," therefore, is a self-limiting mindset; if you think something is impossible, then it becomes so.

Self-Belief and *Real* Leadership

Self-belief among the highest-achieving *real* leaders comprises the following:

---

14. Roger Bannister, *The Four-Minute Mile*, The Lyons Press, 2004, p. viii.

- Belief in their ability to achieve their goals

- Belief in their qualities and abilities

- Belief that they can achieve anything they set their mind to

- Belief that they can punch through any obstacle put in their way

Further, I have found that strong and resilient self-belief is accompanied by a humility that sets these leaders aside from others whose self-belief is more fragile. They rarely take things personally and view any negative feedback they receive as a means of helping them move further onward and upward. They have no need to inform and remind others of their own achievements and abilities because they possess an inner belief that requires no external reinforcement to sustain it. These leaders *do* have doubts from time to time, of course, but this is mainly about their confidence in specific situations, which can actually serve an important purpose in preventing them from becoming complacent.

The deep inner belief these *real* leaders possess enables them to thrive and excel under the pressure of being visible. It drives their desire and ability to:

- Set and achieve stretching goals

- Accept and learn from criticism

- Seek and understand the causes of failure

- Establish a balanced perspective on strengths and weaknesses, and to tackle the weaknesses head-on

- Accept responsibility and accountability when things go wrong

- Take risks

- Make decisions without fear of being wrong

- See mistakes as a key part of their development and learning

- Control potentially debilitating fear

- Bounce back from setbacks with renewed focus and effort

Self-belief is, therefore, one of the key skills underpinning mental toughness in *real* leaders. Fortunately, it is not an attribute that you either have or don't have. It can be worked on and developed to levels that deliver extraordinary performance.

What Is Self-Belief?

Self-belief comprises two specific components: self-esteem and self-confidence.

- Self-esteem is a way of thinking and feeling that implies you accept, respect, and trust yourself. It is developed over time and is unlikely to change much in the short term. It is largely unaffected by the external environment and therefore within your control.

- Self-confidence reflects your optimism about being successful in specific situations and circumstances. This is the part of your belief that is at the mercy of the changing environment. It is more easily and immediately influenced by external conditions so that you are not always in control of it; it can therefore fluctuate significantly over a very short time period. Essentially, you "hand over" your self-confidence to others, or situational conditions, which then determine its level and nature.

Imagine you are delivering a presentation. As you look around at individual faces in the audience, your confidence rises as your gaze falls on someone who is smiling and nodding in agreement with the points you are making. Now imagine what happens to your confidence as your gaze turns to a person whose expression exudes obvious boredom and disinterest, and then to another individual who clearly dislikes or disagrees with what you are saying. How is your confidence affected?

The key to your confidence is that it is dictated by things in the external environment largely outside your control. However, there is also another important predictor of confidence totally within your control: self-esteem. The relationship between self-esteem and self-confidence is shown in Figure 9.1, on the following page. When self-esteem is relatively low, self-confidence fluctuates at a relatively low level; when self-esteem is relatively high, self-confidence still fluctuates, but at a relatively high level.

How does this work in reality? Returning to the example of delivering a presentation, remember that your confidence will be affected by the reaction of individuals in the audience, something you cannot control. What you *can* control is your thinking about the wide and deep knowledge base you have developed over many years on the content of your presentation, and on the positive feedback you have received on your presentation skills on numerous occasions. These are the things that will influence your confidence, if you choose to focus on them.

What Is *Your* Level of Self-Belief?

As a *real* leader, you will not be perfect; nobody is! Like everyone else, you will experience good and bad days, times when things go well and times when things go wrong. Peaks and troughs in your confidence levels will come and go, but your self-esteem

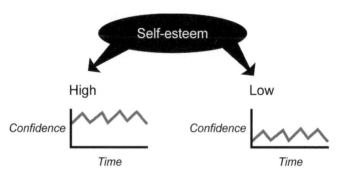

Figure 9.1 The Relationship Between Self-Esteem and Self-Confidence[15]

will be relatively stable. Spend a few minutes reflecting on the questions posed in Time-Out 9 to begin the process of better understanding your belief in yourself.

TIME-OUT 9

WHAT IS *YOUR* LEVEL OF SELF-BELIEF?

- **How much belief do you have in yourself as a *real* leader?**

- **How would you rate your level of self-esteem?**

- **To what extent does your self-confidence fluctuate when you are at work? What specifically affects your self-confidence?**

So Where Do You Start?

Leaders who want to strengthen their self-belief have a tendency to focus on improving their self-confidence. This is where the dis-

---

15. Figure reproduced from G. Jones and A. Moorhouse, *Developing Mental Toughness: Gold Medal Strategies for Transforming Your Business Performance*, Spring Hill, 2008.

tinction between self-esteem and self-confidence becomes especially important. Building self-confidence can be a short-term "fix" that helps leaders deal with specific events and situations, but it does not help them in the long term. My approach is to get them working first on their self-esteem before learning strategies and tools to build their confidence. In this way, as important events get closer they focus more on their ability and what they have achieved over the long term than on factors in the environment they cannot control. The following chapters in this master class therefore focus first on developing and enhancing self-esteem before moving on to self-confidence.

KEY TAKEAWAYS

■ Self-belief is composed of self-esteem and self-confidence.

■ Self-esteem is a way of thinking and feeling that implies that you accept, respect, and trust yourself.

■ Self-esteem is developed over time and is unlikely to alter very much in the short term.

■ Self-confidence reflects your optimism about being successful in specific situations.

■ Self-confidence is dictated by things in the external environment largely outside your control and can fluctuate significantly over a very short time period.

■ When self-esteem is relatively low, self-confidence fluctuates at a relatively low level; when self-esteem is relatively high, self-confidence fluctuates at a relatively high level.

Chapter 10

■ ■ ■

Building Your Self-Esteem

KEY TOPICS

■ **Responding constructively to feedback**
■ **Dealing with successes and failures**
■ **Letting go of perfectionist tendencies**

Do you feel good about yourself as a human being? Do the values that drive the way you lead your life give you a sense of pride? Do you feel good about yourself as a leader? Do the values that drive the way you lead your people give you a sense of pride? Are you aware of what has underpinned your successes to date? Are you proud of your successes to date?

If you responded in the affirmative to the majority of these questions, your self-esteem is likely to be healthy and you are able to go about your role and responsibilities as a *real* leader with a strong foundation for stretching and challenging yourself. Unfortunately, I know leaders who would not respond positively to some of the questions posed above. These are the leaders whose self-esteem is fragile and poses a threat to their aspirations to be *real* leaders. Their visibility can simply overwhelm what relatively little self-esteem they possess.

Give It Time

The most important factor to keep in mind when practicing strategies and tools for enhancing your self-esteem is that it comes from within. The foundation for your perceptions and feelings of self-worth is internal so that how you think and feel about yourself is completely under your control. But I am afraid there is no shortcut to building self-esteem that will be durable and stable. The resilient self-esteem that will help to make you mentally tough will not develop overnight or as a consequence of a single action, thought, decision, or behavioral change. Instead, self-esteem is enhanced gradually and through a number of different strategies and tools described in the following pages.

Avoiding Taking Things Personally

As a *real* leader, the visibility and exposure resulting from your willingness and desire to put yourself on the line means that you will have access to numerous sources of feedback about how people are responding to you and your leadership. There will be formal mechanisms (for example, 360-degree feedback, internal surveys, and performance reviews) as well as more informal means, including things like conversations with colleagues, people's body language during your presentations and meetings you chair, and counsel from your trusted advisors.

Amid this vast array of information regarding what people think about you, there are two important choices open to you in terms of how you contextualize any feedback that is not 100 percent positive:

    1. You can view the feedback as negative and critical, or you can view it as developmental.

2. You can interpret the feedback as being about you as a person, or view it as being about your behavior as a leader.

A combination of choosing to view the feedback as negative and critical and also as being about you as a person will do little for your self-esteem if this is your normal way of responding. This is where you take things personally and lapse into an "I'm no good" thinking pattern. You become very sensitive and begin to read negative intent into other people's words and actions, looking for reinforcement of some insecurity within you. Over time, if not addressed, this way of thinking will dent your self-esteem.

Sadly, some people are just not able to get themselves out of this way of thinking, and it provides a serious obstacle to their careers. I recently came across a leader who had gotten himself into such a downward spiral of suspicion that he was reading negative intent into almost everything his colleagues said and did. His mounting insecurity caused him to challenge his direct reports' innocent comments, somehow turning them into a cunning and devious means of ridiculing him. He denied and resisted any feedback he received as part of the organization's 360 review process and was passed over for promotion on several occasions.

Fortunately, there is an effective alternative if you choose to go down a different path. First, you should view feedback as being developmental or, in other words, that it is provided with the best intentions of the giver as a means of helping you become an even better leader. Second, you should contextualize the feedback as being about your behavior as a leader and not about you as a person. You can modify your behavior quickly, but there will not be much you can do about you as a person.

This mindset was especially effective for one leader I worked with who was a sponge for feedback. She was hungry for any type of feedback on her leadership, and she invited it from all levels in the organization. This lay at the core of her personal growth as a leader, and she developed a reputation for creating a culture of openness and trust that underpinned her rapid progress through the organization.

So the combination of viewing feedback as developmental and also about your behavior as a leader is much more constructive and will actually help you grow not only as a leader, but also in terms of your self-esteem.

Boosting Your Credit Score

Think back to a recent success or a time when things went well for you in your role as a leader. You have 100 points to assign and divide across the four reasons below for your success (note that if you assign 40 points, for example, to your ability in the first statement, then you have another 60 to divide and assign across the remaining three statements):

1. I was successful because of my ability.

2. I was successful because I put in a lot of effort.

3. I was successful because it was relatively easy to succeed.

4. I was successful because I was lucky.

Now think back to a recent failure or a time when things went wrong in your role as a leader. You have another 100 points to assign and divide across the four reasons below for your failure:

1. I failed because of my lack of ability.

2. I failed because I did not try hard enough.

3. I failed because it was difficult to succeed.

4. I failed because I was unlucky.

There may be other reasons for your success or failure than those listed above, but whatever you attribute the causes to, they will fall within two dimensions:

- An internal-external dimension that reflects whether the cause or "source of control" is internal or external to you

- A constant-variable dimension that reflects the degree of "changeability" of the cause

Figure 10.1, on the following page, shows how the four reasons listed above for your success and failure fit into this framework:

- First, your "ability" as a *real* leader is an internal factor under your control, but it is also a constant factor that cannot be changed to any great extent in the short term.

- Second, the amount of "effort" you devote to being a *real* leader is internal since it is under your total control, and it is also variable so you can change how much effort you put in very quickly.

- Third, "difficulty" is external in that it is largely determined by the organizational climate and environment you are leading in, and it is also constant so you can do little to change it.

- Finally, "luck" is clearly external and variable since you have no control over it and it can change rapidly.

Think back to the success and failure you identified earlier and how you divided the 100 points for each. Were the causes predominantly internal or external, or predominantly variable or con-

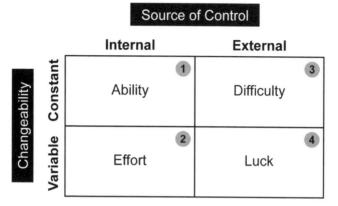

Figure 10.1 How Do You Attribute Success and Failure?[16]

stant? Do you typically attribute causes of success and failure in this way?

Returning to the framework shown in Figure 10.1, it will become evident how your attributions impact on your sense of self-worth as a person and as a leader as each quadrant is described in more detail.

- The *internal-constant quadrant* (1) includes causes such as your ability, expertise, experience, and skills as a leader. These factors are totally under your control and are constant and enduring. If you achieve a success and attribute the cause to one or more of these things, this will give you an enduring sense of pride and competence that will feed your self-esteem. You can essentially feel good about yourself in a way that will not evaporate overnight. The flip side, of course, is that when you attribute failure to things that are internal and constant, you are likely to be down on yourself for reasons that are difficult to change in the short

16. This figure is based on the work of B. Weiner, *Theories of Motivation: From Mechanism to Cognition*, Rand-McNally, 1972.

term. This will be an inevitable threat to your sense of self-worth as a leader. However, it is important to remember that the durable and stable nature of self-esteem means it will take a number of successes or failures to be attributed in this way before self-esteem is significantly affected. In other words, your self-esteem should not be impacted by one very good or very poor performance, but rather by successive events and circumstances that continually reinforce your thoughts and feelings about your self-worth.

- The *internal-variable quadrant* (2) also includes causes that are under your control (e.g., effort, preparation, planning, own attitudes and mindset), but their variable nature means they are likely to have less impact on self-esteem than attributions made in the internal-constant quadrant (1).

- The *external-constant quadrant* (3) includes attributions outside your control that are constant. These are about other people and the environment you are leading in so they should have relatively little impact on your self-esteem (e.g., your team members' capability, quality of your competitors, targets set by others).

- The *external-variable quadrant* (4) also includes causes of success and failure you have no control over but which are variable (e.g., luck, economic climate, competitors' focus and strategy). Again, these attributions should have no impact on your self-esteem since they say nothing about you as a leader.

The takeaway message is that self-esteem can be developed and enhanced by identifying aspects of success that are attributable to your more permanent and enduring attributes, such as your ability and experience as a *real* leader. I have worked with leaders whose relatively low self-esteem has meant they often struggle to take personal credit for their successes. Instead, their successes have occurred because they "were in the right place at the right time," or perhaps they were "part of an outstanding team." Likewise, they often assign failures to their own short-comings and mistakes. For example, I have been coaching one particular managing director with relatively low self-esteem on strategies that will prevent him from apologizing for everything that goes wrong in his organization and giving anyone else bar himself the plaudits for the successes. Much of my work with this particular leader has been working out how he has gotten to the level he is currently operating at and attributing it to internal factors such as ability, skills, etc.

Key to this whole process is ensuring you take appropriate personal credit for your successes and do not distort your attributions of failure in a way that you assume personal responsibility when it is unjustified. Underlying this message is the need to be logical and rational in the way you attribute success and failure. Kidding yourself will serve no long-term benefit and may even prevent you from developing as a *real* leader because you ignore key development areas.

Recalling and Celebrating Your Achievements

How much time do you devote to thinking about your achievements? My guess would be "not much." My second guess is that you often rely on your most recent past experiences to judge how you are doing as a *real* leader. Resilient self-esteem is not based on the last few days, weeks, or even months, but rather on your whole experience as a person and in your career as a leader. Now is your opportunity to spend some time reflecting on your achievements in Time-Out 10.1.

TIME-OUT 10.1

WHAT ARE YOUR ACHIEVEMENTS?

- **Reflect on and list your achievements in life in general.**

- **Reflect on and list your achievements as a leader.**

- **Now return to the lists you have generated and search through your memory to ensure you have listed everything.**

The achievements you have generated should form the foundation of your self-esteem. Remind yourself of them from time to time. Many of the leaders I have coached have listed them on small cards which they keep in their organizers, wallets, or briefcases. They are there for them when they find themselves in pressure situations that threaten their confidence, when factors in the external environment are impacting negatively on their thoughts and feelings. The words on the cards allow them to step back inside themselves in order to regain control and gather strength from their self-esteem.

I encourage you to keep your list of achievements close at hand, too, but they will only be useful if you remind yourself of them from time to time. Use the reminder as a stimulus to also *celebrate* your achievements. You will need to find a way that works for you, but here are a couple of examples to get your creative juices flowing. A couple of people I have worked with have framed their list of achievements and hung it on a wall at home. Another leader chose to mark the anniversary of significant achievements in her calendar so that she could give herself a treat on particular anniversaries, such as receiving her MBA and getting promoted to her current role.

So, as well as reminding yourself of your achievements, do not forget to celebrate them in some way. Finally, always remember that your worth is a function of you as a person and leader and not the circumstances that surround you!

Trying *Not* to Be Perfect

My experience of successful leaders is that virtually all of them have some degree of perfectionism in them. In its simplest form, perfectionism is the tendency to routinely set unrealistically high expectations for yourself and others. Perfectionists also focus on small flaws and shortcomings in themselves and their achievements and ignore or forget what is good about them. I introduced perfectionism in Master Class 2 as being an important contributor to stress. It is also a common cause of reduced self-esteem among leaders whose unrealistic expectations mean that nothing they do is ever good enough; they are highly critical of themselves.

Conquering the negative consequences of perfectionism requires a fundamental shift in your attitude toward yourself and how you approach life and leadership in general. The following strategies and guidelines provide a starting point for this shift:

- **Accepting mistakes.** Leaders with perfectionist tendencies focus on the smallest flaws and mistakes and beat themselves up over them. The best *real* leaders accept they will mess up from time to time. Indeed, learning from making mistakes is an important part of their development. They dwell on mistakes only as long as it takes to draw out the important learning points and then move on to focus on the here-and-now. *Nobody* is perfect, so why should *you* expect to be? You will never achieve this goal.

• **Setting goals that are achievable.** Talking of goals, perfectionists seldom achieve their personal goals because they are so high and unrealistic. This is exacerbated by their reluctance to accept that goals should be set any lower. If you recognize this trait in yourself, the starting point is to identify any constraints on your capacity to achieve these goals, such as time and lack of control over some important factors in the environment, and also personal limitations. You will probably need the help of someone you respect and trust in order to be able to set attainable expectations.

• **Recognizing and overcoming perfectionist thinking styles.** There are three types of thinking styles[17] especially relevant to perfectionism. Do you engage in any of these?

1. **"Should/must" thinking:**
   "I should be able to do this right."
   "I must not mess up."

2. **"All or nothing" thinking:**
   "I can't do this at all."
   "This is completely wrong."

3. **"Overgeneralization" thinking:**
   "I'll never be able to do this."
   "I always get things wrong."

It is particularly important that you recognize such thoughts and self-talk when you are under pressure because this type

---

17. E. J. Bourne, *The Anxiety and Phobia Workbook,* New Harbinger Publications, Oakland, California, 1995.

of thinking exacerbates any negative effects of pressure, with the danger it will turn into stress. Become aware of your use of "should," "must," "never," "have to," and "always" in pressure situations and learn to use more rational and positive counterstatements. The process of changing self-talk is described in the next chapter.

So What Will You Do?

Strengthening your self-esteem, whatever its current level, will benefit you greatly in your role as a *real* leader. It will provide you with the foundation for stretching and challenging yourself, and then bouncing back when you experience the inevitable setbacks. Work through Time-Out 10.2 and identify how you will work on your self-esteem.

TIME-OUT 10.2

BUILDING YOUR SELF-ESTEEM

This chapter has covered the following strategies for developing your self-esteem:

- **Avoiding taking things personally**

- **Boosting your credit score, in the form of how you attribute success and failure**

- **Recalling and celebrating your achievements**

- **Trying *not* to be perfect**

---

continued

Which of these strategies and tools, or elements of different ones, most appeals to you? How do you intend to put it or them into practice?

The strategies and tools described in this chapter have provided a framework within which you can start to enhance your self-esteem. Remember that you will need to work on it gradually, so be patient and stick with it.

KEY TAKEAWAYS

- Self-esteem comes from within and is about how you perceive yourself.
- There is no quick way to building self-esteem; it is enhanced gradually via continual reinforcement of your self-worth.
- Taking things personally will reduce your self-esteem if you persist in it.
- Self-esteem is enhanced when you give yourself credit for your successes.
- Self-esteem is enhanced when you remind yourself of your achievements.
- Self-esteem is likely to be enhanced when you let go of perfectionist tendencies.

Chapter 11

■ ■ ■

Boosting Your Self-Confidence

KEY TOPICS

■ Focusing on your recent achievements and experiences

■ Managing your self-talk and mental rehearsal

■ Interpreting your emotional state in a positive way

As a *real* leader you will find yourself making and owning decisions you may not be sure about. You may find yourself chairing a hurriedly arranged crisis meeting, or being "summoned" to provide an explanation of your team's expensive mistake. You will probably be put on the spot by being asked difficult questions you do not know the answers to, or learn five minutes before a big sales pitch of a serious flaw in your proposal. On occasions like these, you neither have time, nor is it appropriate, to reflect on your worth as a leader; you will find yourself having to bolster or raise your confidence significantly and quickly.

I highlighted earlier in this master class that even the best *real* leaders have self-doubts from time to time when the pressure is most ferocious. This chapter describes a number of strategies and tools these leaders use and that you, too, can employ to regain and enhance confidence levels in the pressure situations you face as a *real* leader.

Focusing on Your Recent Successes

Self-confidence in specific situations is enhanced by focusing on recent successes, say over the past few days, weeks, or perhaps months. This differs from self-esteem, where recalling achievements over a long time frame is more relevant and impactful. What have been your own achievements as a *real* leader over the last few days, weeks, and months? Are you able to remember your successes over the recent past easily, or have you forgotten about them because you are too busy to think about them? Whatever they are, you should not forget them because being able to remind yourself of recent successes when your confidence is becoming a little fragile is an effective tool for bolstering it when under pressure.

You will also have a record of your recent successes in the form of mental images. Try replaying one or two of them and make them as vivid as possible. Imagine all details of the achievement, including what you did and how it made you feel. Imagery is a very powerful tool that can be of enormous benefit. Store these images and replay them to bolster your confidence before important situations.

I have coached leaders who keep a log of their recent successes as a constant reminder of what they have done well. They update them regularly, including details of what they did and how it made them feel.

Ensuring "Quick Wins"

You will probably have long-term goals related to your ambitions, but have you broken them down into medium- and short-term goals? I encourage leaders who lack confidence to identify short-term goals because if and when they are achieved, they are an important and regular source of confidence. Some of these leaders use their logs to record short-term goals whose achievement will form the foundation of their confidence in the future.

Set some short-term goals for yourself. For example, work out how you will tackle, in the next few days, some of those things you have been avoiding. Set a simple goal of making appointments to have the tricky conversations you have been putting off but so need to have. Figure out times next week that you will set aside for those potentially awkward performance reviews that have been on your to-do list for the past month. These "quick wins" may only be small, but they will build your confidence and also reduce the length of your to-do list. They will also allow you to build up a store of recent successes that you may wish to record on a small card and carry around with you for use when you need a confidence boost.

Drawing on Your Experiences

It will be clear by now that confidence is determined by the situation you find yourself in, which means that it can be enhanced via reflecting on your own recent and positive experiences of situations similar to those you are about to experience. This involves identifying the characteristics of situations you anticipate will be pressured before you actually encounter them. Some or all of the following questions will help you piece together the details of what to expect:

- Who will be involved?

- How many people will be there?

- What do you know about them?

- How do they normally respond?

- What will the physical environment be like?

- Have you performed in the same physical environment before?

- What usually helps you perform at your best?

Identify the things you did well on those previous occasions and the learning points to take forward into upcoming situations. There may be things you associate with success in those situations, such as preparing in a specific way or adopting a particular mindset. Try to recall them so you will be able to repeat them to give your confidence a boost.

Mental Rehearsal

This tool builds on the "Drawing on Your Experiences" section above and is based on the principle that you can create and deal with pressure situations in your mind before you encounter them physically. I have coached leaders who have learned to mentally rehearse difficult conversations with colleagues beforehand. You can do this too. First, identify what you have done well in circumstances like these in the past—how you dealt with the different responses of the people you were talking to, how you remained composed, how you managed to turn a difficult conversation into a productive outcome.

Now, think about a difficult conversation you will need to have with a colleague in the near future. Who is that person? Conjure up a picture of him or her in your mind. How do you normally feel and behave in his or her presence? How does that individual behave with you? What is the issue you need to address? How will you start the conversation? How will that person respond? How will you respond? What will be a good outcome of the conversation?

The next stage is to work through the conversation in your mind. See and hear yourself saying the words you will open up the conversation with. Imagine staying calm and composed as you make your points clearly and precisely. Imagine giving your colleague time and space to respond. Imagine what he or she will say in response to the various points you make. Imagine working through the process until you reach a productive outcome. Now, sit back, close your eyes, and have a go.

These directions are merely to provide you with an idea of what you can achieve through mental rehearsal. You should find a version that works for you, but try to stick with the basic principles.

Learning from Others

Learning from other people's successes is another way of enhancing your confidence. Observe them carefully in situations where you may struggle with your own confidence. Pick out the things that contributed to their success, and focus on enacting them yourself. Other leaders you consider to be good role models can be particularly important in this respect. You will have watched and listened to them over a prolonged period. How do they enhance their confidence in pressure situations? Why not talk to them about it?

Positive Self-Talk

As I described in Chapter 7, self-talk can be so automatic you do not notice it or the effect it has on your moods and emotions. Self-talk reduces your confidence when it is negative and irrational. "I'm no good," for example, is both negative and irrational for a leader who has reached a senior level. The key to using positive self-talk to boost your confidence is to first slow down and examine the content of your self-talk and how it makes you feel.

Self-talk prominent in people who are prone to low confidence can be broken down into three types:[18]

1. **The worrier.** Typical of the worrier's self-talk is "What if . . . ?" The worrier is characterized by anticipating the worst, overestimating the chances of something bad occurring, and creating images of disastrous failure.

18. E. J. Bourne, *The Anxiety and Phobia Workbook*, New Harbinger Publications, Oakland, California, 1995.

2. **The critic.** Typical of the critic's self-talk is "You're so dumb" and "Can't you ever get it right?" The critic in you constantly judges and evaluates your behavior. It draws attention to your flaws and limitations and pounces on any mistake you make to remind you that you *are* a failure.

3. **The victim.** Typical self-talk engaged in by the victim includes "I'll never be able to do that, so what's the point in trying?" and "Nothing ever goes right." The victim is that part of you that feels helpless or hopeless and believes you are in some way deprived. The victim always sees insurmountable problems between you and your goals and moans and complains about how unfair things are.

Dealing with negative self-talk involves countering it with positive, helpful statements. This involves writing down and rehearsing positive counterstatements and then practicing them. There are four rules for using positive self-talk to counter negative thoughts:

1. The positive statements should directly refute or invalidate your negative self-talk.

2. Avoid negatives. Instead of saying "I'm not going to get stressed by this situation," try "I am confident and calm about this situation."

3. Use the present tense. Instead of saying "I'll be okay in a few minutes," try "I'm okay."

4. Believe what you are saying to yourself. Only use self-talk that has personal credibility for you.

Negative self-talk represents self-limiting mental habits that need to be broken by recognizing occasions when you are experiencing them, and then replacing them with positive self-talk.

Some examples will be helpful here. Imagine a leader who is about to deliver a tough message about the decision to downsize, during which she will ask for people to come forward who are interested in voluntary redundancy. A self-statement such as "I feel so guilty about asking people to do this" will probably not instill much confidence in this leader beforehand. It will probably also betray her true feelings through her body language and the words used at a time when she needs to be strong and resolute. A more helpful self-statement would be "I'm doing what's right for the organization and the people." This will help her feel more confident in delivering the message and, consequently, have an impact on how it is received. In another context, think about how a thought such as "I always get out-maneuvered in these tough budget negotiations" will make anyone feel going into a meeting with his or her peers. "I'm on the ball and have every base covered" is a much more positive mindset to approach this type of situation.

I mentioned earlier that a number of leaders I coach keep logs of their recent achievements and short-term goals. Those who are particularly prone to negative self-talk use the log to identify their typical negative self-statements along with positive counterstatements that are a reminder of how they can rebuild their confidence when necessary.

Interpreting Your Emotional State in a Positive Way

Think about times when you have found yourself in high-pressure situations and your nervousness has become excessive. Your mind is racing and seemingly out of control, your heart is pounding, and you cannot sit still. How does this intense response affect your confidence?

I coached the new managing director of a project management company who told me how he got very nervous in the few minutes before his town hall presentations and how it reduced his confidence. I told him a story about a top 100-meter sprinter who approached me about the almost overwhelming nature of her physical response in the final minutes before a race. She de-scribed how her body tightened up, how her heart pounded, and how she just could not compose herself. She asked me to teach her relaxation tools that would calm her down. I told her I could do this if that is what she *really* wanted, but first we talked about her physical response in relation to the demands of the race. We identified the quick reaction to the starting gun and the explosion out of the blocks that was so crucial. We talked about the power and strength required during those few seconds that comprised her performance. She was quickly able to see how her body was actually preparing itself for achieving those demands and that any relaxation strategy I taught her might decrease her physical readiness. We worked, instead, on how she would reinterpret her physical response as helping her so that she learned to welcome the nervousness she had previously dreaded.

The managing director always recalled this story in his mind be-fore his town hall presentations. He recognized he had a choice about how he thought about his nervousness prior to these pre-sentations: he could see it as working against him, or he could view it as helping him. Not only did this help his confidence, it also improved the quality and impact of his presentations.

This process of being able to positively interpret what may be a very intense mental and physical response to pressure may, in the early stages of practicing this tool, require you to use self-talk to convince yourself, for example, that a pounding heart is a positive sign of readiness before a difficult meeting. The key message is to view and use your response to pressure in a positive way rather than to fight against it.

So What Will You Do?

Self-confidence is different from self-esteem—you can do some-thing about it almost immediately. Spend some time working through Time-Out 11 so you have some strategies and tools to boost your confidence when required.

TIME-OUT 11

BOOSTING YOUR SELF-CONFIDENCE

This chapter has covered the following strategies and tools for boosting your self-confidence:

- Focusing on your recent successes

- Ensuring "quick wins"

- Drawing on your experiences

- Mental rehearsal

- Learning from others

- Positive self-talk

- Interpreting your emotional state in a positive way

Which of these strategies and tools, or elements of different ones, most appeals to you? How do you intend to put it or them into practice?

It is important that you pay particular attention to the images you conjure up and the self-talk you engage in when under pressure because they are likely to have a big impact on your level of confidence. Try experimenting with the strategies and tools described in this chapter and find out what works for you.

KEY TAKEAWAYS

- Self-confidence is different from self-esteem; it can be enhanced quickly via the use of specific strategies and tools.
- Self-confidence can be enhanced by focusing on your recent successes.
- Setting and achieving short-term goals will ensure "quick wins" that will increase your confidence.
- Recalling the things you have done well in your recent experiences of situations similar to the one you are about to encounter will increase your confidence.
- You can create and deal with upcoming pressure situations in your mind via the use of mental rehearsal.
- Observing how others succeed in similar situations can help build your confidence.
- Recognizing self-defeating self-talk and identifying positive counterthoughts will help enhance your confidence.
- Self-confidence can be enhanced by interpreting signs of nervousness in a positive way.

That Concludes Master Class 3

This is the conclusion of Master Class 3. You should now have some strategies and tools that you will use to boost your self-confidence when the situations in which you find yourself are beginning to get on top of you. However, remember it is your self-esteem that will ultimately form the foundation of your ability to thrive on the pressure of being a *real* leader.

Master Class 4

■■■

Channeling Your Motivation to Work *for* You in Your Role as a *Real* Leader

OBJECTIVES

■ To help you better understand the nature and impact of your motivation to be a *real* leader

■ To enlighten you on the key differences between internal and external motivation and how they relate to being a *real* leader

■ To enable you to optimize your motivation to be a *real* leader through setting effective goals

■■■

Chapter 12

■ ■ ■

Ensuring Your Motivation
Is "Healthy"

KEY TOPICS

■ Motivation and *real* leadership
■ Level versus nature of motivation
■ Gaining control over your motivation

There is a common misconception about motivation. Consider two leaders who are both talented and highly motivated to do a great job. The assumption would normally be that both will perform to the best of their impressive ability. But this assumption is inaccurate because their high levels of motivation are experienced in very different ways. One of the leaders really enjoys and thrives on challenge and looks forward to going into the office every day. This leader exudes an infectious enthusiasm that underpins an environment where high performance is inevitable and sustainable. The other one has equally high motivation, but it is in the form of a desperation to succeed. This leader lies awake at night worrying about the threats to personal ambitions that will be encountered the following day. This leader is constrained by a fear of failing that is an obstacle to creating a high-performance environment.

The implication for you as a leader is that it is not simply being highly motivated that will help you to recover from setbacks and enable you to keep going and thrive when the pressure is most fierce. High motivation can actually work against you if it is in the form of desperation, fear, or an obsession with being successful.

This chapter guides you through some key aspects of your own motivation and describes how you can ensure that it works *for* rather than *against* you.

Healthy and Unhealthy Motivation

High motivation in some leaders can take the form of an obsession with being successful. The pressure these leaders place on themselves is enormous, and there is an "unhealthy" aspect to their motives. They are willing to make big sacrifices to achieve their ambitions. I described in Master Class 2 how viewing yourself as making "sacrifices" can cause stress and how making "choices" helps to alleviate stress. "Sacrifices" and "choices" are also important in the context of motivation.

The very best leaders I have worked with do not view themselves as making "sacrifices" because they know this is not a good foundation for their longer-term motivation and ability to thrive on pressure. Instead, they are keen to emphasize the "choices" they have made. For example, if they viewed the time their overnight business trips kept them away from loved ones as a sacrifice, then their longer-term motivation would be in jeopardy. These leaders are capable of extraordinary commitment because they have *chosen* to do so and know how far to take it; it is not something they *must* do at any cost. Theirs is a "healthy" motivation that forms a critical element in enabling them to rebound from setbacks and disappointments because they are able to put things in perspective. They view setbacks as part of their continued development rather than seeing them as disasters that threaten their aspirations.

Exploring the Foundations of Your Motivation

Motivation is not just a day-to-day drive toward achieving carefully planned end goals. It is about your very existence and what you stand for; it is your reason for being. Therefore, you should take regular time-outs to reflect on what is driving you as a leader and why, and adjust the foundations of your motives if necessary.

Motivation is a fundamental driving force behind people's behavior and performance. This section explores a series of basic dimensions of motivation that will help you understand the foundations of your own motivation.

Being Motivated for the Right Reasons

At the most fundamental level, behavior can be divided into two different types: "approach" and "avoidance":

- "Approach" behavior is where you quite literally approach or move toward some set of circumstances.

- "Avoidance" behavior, on the other hand, is where you avoid or move away from a set of circumstances.

These behaviors are underpinned and driven by "approach" and "avoidance" motivation respectively.

This distinction lies at the core of the difference between *real* and *safe* leaders. *Safe* leaders avoid tackling underperformance, while *real* leaders address it head-on. *Safe* leaders are fearful of making mistakes and so avoid putting themselves in situations where they might make them. *Real* leaders, on the other hand, willingly take risks knowing they are accountable if things go wrong. *Safe* leaders sweep failure under the carpet in the hope they can avoid the consequences, while *real* leaders have the courage and desire to seek to understand the causes of failure.

The distinction between approach and avoidance motivation is also evident in other aspects of a leader's behavior. I have coached a number of leaders who have decided that the time has come to look for another job. Classic approach motives underpinning their decision include concluding that they have reached a plateau in their development and need the challenge of a new role in a different type of organization. Or it may be the natural next step to achieving their career ambitions. Having planned their future, these leaders have very healthy motives for moving on.

Leaders driven by avoidance motives, on the other hand, often tell me about being worn down by frustrations in their current role, the inadequacies of some of the people they work with, or perhaps the lack of vision in the organization. They have become disillusioned and want to get away at the earliest opportunity. Often, they believe things will be different elsewhere, but may not be sure what they want to move to; their main motive is to move away from their current environment. These are unhealthy motives for leaving their job, and these leaders sometimes find themselves in new jobs they find are equally, if not more, disappointing. They have spent too much time focusing on what they have and the things they do not like about it, and not enough time focusing on the future and what they want.

What is the main driver of *your* motivation as a *real* leader? Think about your day-to-day motivation as well as your longer-term goals to better understand how you approach or avoid particular aspects of your role as a *real* leader. Pressure that becomes excessive and results in stress can drive avoidance motivation, so reflect in particular on how your motives might change at times when you are stressed.

"Scooby Doo and Scooby Don't Doo" Motivation

I hope you do not mind, but I am going to draw a comparison between you and dogs! Experiments conducted with laboratory dogs a number of years ago revealed intriguing findings that can be applied to leaders.[19] The experiments involved administering shocks to three dogs under different conditions:

- The first dog, which I will call Muttley, was able to turn off the shocks by pushing a panel with its nose.

- The second dog—I will call this one Scooby Doo—was given exactly the same shocks as Muttley, but had no means of escaping them.

- The third dog, which I will name Lassie, did not receive any shocks.

Following this, the dogs were placed in a box with two compartments divided by a low barrier. When the shocks were administered, all Muttley, Scooby Doo, and Lassie had to do to escape them was to jump over the barrier from one compartment to the other. Within seconds, Muttley, who had discovered he could

---

19. M. Seligman, *Learned Optimism: How to Change Your Mind and Your Life*, Pocket Books, 1998.

control the shocks, found that when he jumped over the barrier he escaped them. Lassie, who had received no shocks at all, also discovered quickly that she could get away from the shocks by hopping over the barrier. Scooby Doo, who had found that nothing he did had any effect, made no effort to escape; he lay down even though he continued to receive shocks. Scooby Doo never discovered he could escape the shocks by simply jumping over a small barrier.

Scooby Doo's behavior was driven by "learned helplessness." He had learned that nothing he did could make a difference to the circumstances he found himself in, so why try? Scooby Doo had become "Scooby Don't Doo"! There may have been times when you have felt like giving up because nothing you did seemed to make any difference, so why bother, and why care?

Learned helplessness represents an unhealthy form of motivation. Probably the closest thing to learned helplessness among leaders is the potential for burnout. Burnout is a state of emotional, mental, and physical exhaustion caused by excessive and prolonged stress. This is something that *real* leaders need to be aware, and also wary, of. The pressures of *real* leadership, particularly in turbulent times, can be relentless, and burnout can creep up on you. One of the classic symptoms of burnout is losing interest and not caring anymore. Disengagement, apathy, acquiescence, passiveness, detachment, and feeling worn out are all symptoms associated with this unhealthy form of motivation. It is an unpleasant and sometimes destructive state to be in.

Are there times when *you* stop caring and just "don't give a damn anymore"? Do you disengage from your people and/or situations? Stay alert and vigilant for early signs! If you are able to catch it in its early stages, the stress control strategies and tools described in Master Class 2 will help.

Enjoying Your Motivation

For some leaders, the achievement of their goals and ambitions is so important that they are unable to enjoy their quest to fulfil them. This is typically the case for *safe* leaders whose fear of failure and making mistakes drives their motivation. For these leaders, motivation and self-imposed pressure are the same thing. And this can lead to quite intense symptoms of stress when goals are not achieved. At the extreme, this form of unhealthy motivation turns into an obsession with and desperation for success; anything less is utter failure.

Leaders who are driven by healthy motives enjoy a very different experience. These are the *real* leaders whose goals are challenging but always realistic, ensuring that they are stretching themselves constantly, but not to the breaking point. Their goals are the result of careful reflection about what they are capable of; they are broken down into shorter-term goals and milestones that instill a sense of achievement as they see themselves moving forward. Their motivation underpins an energy and exhilaration that drives them to continuous improvement as they thrive on the pressure of being a *real* leader.

So how much do *you* "enjoy" your own motivation? Do you go to bed at night looking forward to the challenges of the day ahead? Or do you lie awake at night worrying about the threats to your ambitions you will encounter the following day?

Motivating Yourself Inside and Outside

Let me tell you a story about an old man who was very happy with the new house he had just moved to. The quiet street on which it was located, along with the tall brick wall that ran the length of the front garden, provided the privacy and peace he had longed for as he got older.

One day the old man was woken from his afternoon snooze by the noise of a group of kids playing soccer outside his house. The thuds of the soccer ball striking the wall and the shrieks from the kids in celebration of scoring goals were just too much for him. The old man went out to the kids and asked them to play farther down the street. One of the kids responded, "Sorry but we've been playing soccer here after school for a long time now. Your wall makes a perfect goal, and we really enjoy playing here." The old man thought for a few moments and then asked, "If I give you each fifty cents, will you please go and play farther down the street?" The kids agreed reluctantly, and the old man went inside to resume his afternoon rest.

At the same time on the following afternoon, the old man again heard the ball banging loudly against his wall. He went outside and offered the kids fifty cents to play farther down the street. They refused, reminding him that they got particular pleasure from playing in that location because the wall provided such a good goal. The old man then offered them seventy-five cents each to play farther down the street, and they agreed reluctantly to move on.

At the same time on the following day, the old man was yet again woken by the noise of the kids playing soccer outside his house. He went outside and this time had to pay them a dollar each to move on from the place where they so enjoyed playing after school.

The day after that the kids were, for the fourth consecutive day, playing soccer outside the house, but this time the old man failed to appear. The kids went up to the house and knocked on the front door. The old man appeared and the kids said, "Haven't you noticed we're playing soccer outside your house? Why haven't you come out and paid us to move on?" The old man replied, "Yes, I heard you, but I can't pay you. I have no money." The kids responded in disgust, "If that's the case, there's no point in playing outside your house. We'll play farther down the street."

This story reflects a basic distinction between "internal" and "external" motivation, as well as demonstrating how the nature of motivation can change in response to the rewards available to people. The original motivation of the kids was internal in the form of the enjoyment they got from playing soccer against the old man's wall, which provided such a perfect goal. However, this internal motivation was eroded and eventually destroyed by the gradual increases in external motivation the old man provided in the form of money to play farther down the street. Eventually, the point was reached that when the old man ran out of money, there was no internal motivation remaining. They were not playing because they enjoyed it anymore; instead, they were playing for money.

This type of situation is more common in business than you probably think, where it is assumed that external rewards will drive people's performance. And of course this is often the case, but issues arise when internal motivation is eroded as a consequence. Organizations that incentivize their employees through substantial bonuses for hitting performance targets are effectively controlling these employees' motivation. In fact, people's external motivation is increased to the extent that their internal motivation reduces to the point where they become too heavily dependent on those material incentives to keep going. High levels of external motivation can also drive quite extreme behaviors in the quest to gain those rewards, resulting in stress and potential burnout, as well as unhealthy competition with colleagues.

Where does *your* motivation to be a *real* leader come from? Is it driven internally by your own pride, enjoyment, interest, satisfaction, and general desire to do the best job possible? Or is it more in line with *safe* leadership where your motivation is driven by your desire for the external rewards and incentives on offer?

Internal Motivation, External Motivation, and *Real* Leadership

The critical significance of the internal-external dimension of motivation and how it relates to being able to thrive on the pressure of *real* leadership warrants deeper examination. First, we need to be clear about the difference between internal and external motivation:

- *External* motivation drives involvement in an activity in order to attain some outcome separable from the activity. In the context of leadership, those leaders who place more emphasis on the tangible incentives (salary, bonus, etc.) received for doing a good job are externally motivated.

- *Internal* motivation, on the other hand, refers to being involved in an activity for the inherent satisfaction derived from the activity itself. In other words, leaders who are driven more by the enjoyment they derive from being a leader than the "package" they receive are more internally motivated.

Master Class 1 described how *safe* and *real* leaders are driven by different motives. Essentially, *safe* leaders are more externally motivated than internally motivated. They are driven so much by their need for rewards, status, and power that they are unwilling to put themselves on the line because of the threat of losing their position if they get it wrong. *Safe* leaders are fearful of making mistakes because of the implications they might have for their security. They are therefore reluctant to be under the spotlight.

These leaders crave recognition for achievements they may not be responsible for but will claim the credit anyway. They will be driven by the next bonus and what that will allow them to purchase—the next expensive car, the second holiday home—that will provide them with another material possession that will make them feel good about themselves.

Real leaders, on the other hand, are more internally motivated than externally motivated. They are driven much more by the enjoyment they derive from putting themselves out there and making a difference; this is what leadership is about for them. *Real* leaders see mistakes as a key part of their development. They accept that they are highly visible.

These leaders take pride from seeing their people grow as a result of the development opportunities they have provided. They enjoy seeing their people receive the credit they deserve for their hard efforts. Their next new car is chosen because it is something they enjoy driving and have no interest in the impression it sends to others.

There are differences in both well-being and performance in *real* leaders whose motivation is internal compared to those *safe* leaders who are externally motivated. Research by Richard Ryan and Edward Deci[20] indicates that:

---

20. R. Ryan and E. Deci, "Self-determination theory and the facilitation of intrinsic motivation, social development and well-being," *American Psychologist*, 2000, 68–78.

- A strong focus on internal motives, such as personal growth and development as a leader, is associated with higher self-esteem and self-actualization and lower stress.

- On the other hand, a strong focus on satisfying external motives, such as the wealth and profile that can be achieved as a leader, is associated with lower self-esteem and self-actualization and higher stress.

- It is not merely the "focus" on internal and external motives that is important; the "attainment" of these different aspirations has essentially the same effect on well-being.

- Internally motivated *real* leaders, when compared to externally motivated *safe* leaders, demonstrate greater persistence, creativity, energy, well-being, and, crucially, performance.

Given the obvious importance of being internally motivated as a leader, let us take a closer look at how internal motivation can be maximized.

Maximizing Internal Motivation

Internal motivation is reflected in the value you place on personal growth as a *real* leader and your desire to seek out new challenges so that you can extend your leadership skills. It drives an energy and enjoyment that is an important resource for *real* leaders, helping them thrive on pressure rather than being swallowed up by it. Ryan and Deci's work shows that for internal motivation to be maintained, enhanced, and eventually maximized, it is necessary to satisfy three innate psychological needs essential for your health and well-being:

1. Competence: a feeling of mastery or accomplishment as a leader

2. Autonomy: a sense of being in control over your behavior as a leader

3. Relatedness: a sense of belonging, in this case to your organization, business unit, or team

The satisfaction of these needs at work results in increased well-being and higher performance than when it is not experienced. The fluctuation of the satisfaction of these needs on a daily basis also predicts mood, vitality, and self-esteem.[21] Do I have to say any more about the importance of internal motivation to *real* leaders?

Some of the strategies for achieving greater internal motivation in the environment you operate in include:

• Finding ways of feeling competent as a leader

• Ensuring that you exercise choice over your leadership behavior

• Relating in some positive way to the people you lead

• When goals are externally imposed, making sure that you identify short-term goals and milestones that help you to monitor progress on a regular basis, thus gradually building your feeling of competence as a leader

---

21. M. Gagne and E. Deci, "Self-determination theory and work motivation," *Journal of Organizational Behavior*, 2005, 331–362.

- Seeking regular feedback on your leadership development that will similarly provide a means of monitoring your progress

- Working hard at getting to know your colleagues as people and not just team members

Before you get too carried away with your determination to maximize your internal motivation, let me bring you back to reality. It is unrealistic and inappropriate in most leadership contexts for you to be purely internally motivated. The stakes are simply too high for leaders to be permitted to pursue their personal needs solely for interest and enjoyment. But you *can* focus on achieving an optimal *degree* of internal motivation appropriate to your specific situation.

So What Will You Do?

Motivation is complex, and I have tried to reduce it to its most user-friendly forms in this chapter. Use Time-Out 12 to help you

---

TIME-OUT 12

IS YOUR MOTIVATION HEALTHY?

- **Is your motivation to be a leader driven more by approach or avoidance motives?**

- **Are there times when you feel helpless?**

---

continued

- Do you enjoy your motivation, or does it cause you stress?

- Is your motivation to be a leader driven more by internal or external motives?

- What do you need to work on to maximize the healthiness of your motivation?

figure out how you need to work, not only on your *level* of motivation but, more important, on the *nature* of your motivation.

Motivation is the driving force behind your behavior. However, its healthy and unhealthy dimensions mean that your motivation needs to be channeled carefully to allow you to thrive on pressure. The following chapter describes how setting effective goals will help you achieve this.

KEY TAKEAWAYS

- It is not the "level" but rather the "nature" of motivation that is more important in driving behavior.
- Motivation can be healthy or unhealthy.
- *Safe* leaders are driven more by avoidance motivation in the form of fear, while *real* leaders are driven more by approach motivation in the form of desire.
- Learned helplessness is a sign of burnout.

- *Safe* leaders are driven more by external motivation, while *real* leaders are driven more by internal motivation.
- Internally motivated *real* leaders, when compared to externally motivated *safe* leaders, demonstrate greater persistence, creativity, energy, well-being, and, crucially, performance.
- There are three innate psychological needs essential to your health and well-being as a *real* leader: competence, autonomy, and relatedness.

Chapter 13

■ ■ ■

Channeling Your Motivation
into Goals

KEY TOPICS

■ **Goal setting and internal motivation**
■ **"INSPIRED" goals**
■ **Outcome, performance, and process goals**

Goal setting has been touched upon in previous master classes as being an important part of the process of developing the mental toughness *real* leaders require. This chapter takes a detailed look at goal setting because it is so inextricably linked to motivation and being a *real* leader.

Why Set Goals?

All leaders have goals they want to achieve, but not all of them are aware of what they are. These leaders have not been through the process of detailed reflection and identification of what they want to achieve in their careers. These are the leaders who become easily derailed under pressure as they lack a specific frame of reference to harness their focus. The very best leaders set long-term goals and then plan aligned shorter-term goals in a structured and meticulous fashion. Goals give clarity and meaning to these *real* leaders' efforts and drive persistence in the most arduous circumstances. Goals underpin the discipline and determination *real* leaders require to deal with adversity and bounce back after failure. They provide a focus for *real* leaders who might otherwise become distracted under pressure. And they provide a huge sense of confidence when they are achieved.

It is not sufficient, however, to merely set goals. Their nature is critical because not all goals are effective and some can actually be dysfunctional. A fine dividing line exists between setting goals that are just about achievable, but have a level of uncertainty that sustains motivation, focus, and effort, and unattainable goals that actually add to the already intense pressure *real* leaders may be under. Such goals are ultimately demotivating and counterproductive.

The following sections describe the key essentials of setting effective goals, along with frameworks that provide you with a means of structuring and planning them to maximize their effectiveness.

The Key Essentials of Effective Goals

I am sure you already know about the key essentials of setting goals. Unfortunately, leaders often forget to put them all into practice when setting their own or others' goals. For goals to be effective, they need to satisfy the criteria described below:

- Effective goals are **INTERNALIZED**. It does not matter who has set your goals, you have to own and commit to them.

- Effective goals are **NURTURING**. They should include a developmental element so that significant learning occurs in addition to the targets being achieved.

- Effective goals are **SPECIFIC**. They are clear and unambiguous so that it is obvious when they have been achieved.

- Effective goals are **PLANNED**. You should break them down into aligned shorter-term goals, or subgoals, and form a plan for achieving them.

- Effective goals are **IN YOUR CONTROL**. Their achievement should be attainable through your own efforts.

- Effective goals are **REVIEWED REGULARLY**. Regular reviews of progress toward them should be included in the planning process.

- Effective goals are **ENERGIZING**. They should excite and energize you by being challenging in that they are just about achievable, but should also create a level of uncertainty that sustains your motivation, focus, and effort.

- Effective goals are **DOCUMENTED**. Documenting them in some form and recording progress toward them provides a continual reminder of commitments that can be important when things are tough.

You may have figured out already that I have deliberately represented the criteria to fit the acronym INSPIRED.

Documented
Energizing
Reviewed regularly
In your control
Planned
Specific
Nurturing
Internalized

This is what effective goals do; they *inspire* you to achieve them.

INSPIRED Goals in Action

An example of a leader who applied the INSPIRED goal-setting framework to good effect is provided by Nancy, a director of talent development in a financial services firm. Nancy had received feedback on one member of her team, Ed, which suggested that he had been slow in responding to requests for support from a number of individuals in the talent pool. Ed's annual performance review was on the horizon, and she brought it forward a couple of weeks.

During the review, it dawned on Nancy that Ed's lack of urgency was the result of his changed attitude—he had lost his previous strong commitment to the role. He had been in the same role for a couple of years and had simply lost energy for it. They talked about his aspirations and the possibilities of moving to a role he would find more challenging. Ed had a lot to offer the organization, and Nancy was keen to support his development. But first she needed to be convinced that his attitude would not cause more problems in the future.

Nancy employed the INSPIRED framework to set goals that would form the foundation of Ed's development. Specifically, following the essential elements resulted in the following process:

> **Internalized:** There were three aspects of the goal-setting process that enabled Ed to internalize and own his goals. First, Nancy clarified with Ed what his ultimate goal was in the next 12 months. Ed was clear that it was to be ready to move into a more challenging role. Second, Nancy asked Ed to rate on a 1 ("not at all") to 10 ("extremely") scale how motivated he was to achieve the ultimate goal of moving into

a more challenging role. He rated his level of motivation to achieve it as a 10. Third, having both agreed that Ed's attitude was the general source of his underperformance, Nancy asked him to identify the specific elements of this attitude that needed to change and then to construct the words that would best reflect the goal he was trying to achieve. The goal he generated was "to stay in the game." The important thing about using Ed's own words for this goal was that he generated and owned them, and they had a very precise meaning to him: stay focused and committed to my role.

Nurturing: Nancy was pleased with this "stay in the game" goal because she knew it would help Ed not just over the next few months, but also throughout his whole career. It had precise meaning for what he needed to do to achieve his next, more challenging position, but it was also generic enough to refocus him when necessary.

Specific: Nancy then asked Ed to identify some specific actions associated with his "stay in the game" goal. He identified two that he would focus on. First, he would make contact with talent pool individuals who requested his support within 24 hours of receiving the initial request. Second, he would have regular one-on-ones with talent pool members to ascertain their development needs going forward.

Planned: Nancy wanted to ensure that Ed had a plan for achieving the goals he had set. For example, what would he need to do to be able to guarantee a 24-hour response commitment? Part of the plan to achieve this was that he would leave time aside during every working day to react to requests. Specifically, he would mark a two-hour slot in his calendar as "leave free." He would also document the one-on-ones with talent pool members at least two months in advance.

In your control: Nancy was keen that Ed was in control over achieving his goals. She knew, for example, that some talent pool individuals would be resistant to meeting with Ed on a regular basis. They talked about how Nancy could support Ed in getting their buy-in and commitment to the process and concluded that a communication from her to the pool explaining the importance of these sessions would help. They eventually arrived at a goal of 80 percent success rate in holding one-on-ones as realistic and in Ed's control.

Reviewed regularly: Ed's enthusiasm for his role had already waned once, and Nancy wanted to ensure that this would not happen again. Rather than wait for the next formal stage in the performance review process, they agreed to meet to review progress once every other week for the first six weeks and then once a month thereafter.

Energizing: Ed was fully aware that his goal of "staying in the game" was daunting to achieve over a sustained period. But Nancy was assured that his ultimate goal of moving into a more challenging role excited him and would keep him going in the face of any setbacks.

Documented: Ed's goals were, of course, formally documented in his Personal Development Plan that would sit in the company's files. However, Nancy also encouraged Ed to write them down in a small notebook which he could use as a continual reminder, and also use as a log to record progress.

Achieving these goals was by no means an easy task for Ed, and there *were* some setbacks along the way. But the framework Nancy had followed in establishing the goals and the process she facilitated along the way enabled Ed to move into a challenging role with more responsibility. Someone who could so easily have been lost to the organization was now an important contributor to its future growth.

Outcome, Performance, and Process Goals

I will use a sports metaphor to explain the difference between outcome, performance, and process goals. If you ask a world top-ten golfer what his goal is for the tournament next week, he will likely tell you that he "wants to win." This is quite natural, of course, but the problem is that there will be over a hundred golfers starting the tournament and only one of them can win it. If the golfer fails to win, he has failed to achieve his goal. Golfers playing at this level have more than one goal, of course, because they know they cannot win every tournament they compete in.

The goal "to win" is an "outcome" goal because it targets a specific outcome. As shown in Table 13.1, the outcome is not within the golfer's control. He could play brilliantly, but come in second to another golfer who has performed even more outstandingly. Because of the lack of control and the strong desire to achieve them, outcome goals create pressure that has the potential to turn into stress.

The golfer in question will therefore set two other types of goals, both of which are under his total control. The example of a "performance" goal the golfer might set is his own score after the four rounds that comprise his performance in the tournament. In this example, he has figured out that, given the course conditions and weather forecast, 10 under par should be a good enough score to win this particular tournament. This is completely under his control and causes less pressure than the "win" goal. Underpinning the golfer's performance goal are "process" goals. The examples "smooth swing" and "stay focused" are again completely under his control, have little pressure associated with them, and underpin the achievement of his performance goal.

Outcome	Performance	Process
Refers to a performance outcome	Refers to the performance under-pinning the outcome	Refers to the pro-cesses underpinning the performance
Example: *Win the tournament*	*Example:* *10 under par over* *four rounds*	*Examples:* *Smooth swing* *Stay focused*
Not under your control	Under your total control	Under your total control
High pressure	Less pressure	Less pressure

Table 13.1 Outcome, Performance, and Process Goals

An important factor in planning goals is to ensure the three different types of goals are planned and aligned toward the same ends. I used a sports example above to highlight how the different types of goals fit together, but the process is also a powerful tool for use in the business world. Figure 13.1 shows how a sales team leader in a large insurance company defined an outcome goal as winning the prestigious annual Sales Team of the Year internal award.

The team was competing against all the other sales teams in the company and, therefore, not in control of this outcome. What the team *was* in control of was its performance over the year; following consultation with team members, the leader arrived at a performance goal of bettering their previous year's numbers by 15 percent. The leader identified some key process goals underpinning this improvement: specifically, they would focus on improving their telephone rapport-building skills, they would work

Figure 13.1 Planning and Aligning Outcome, Performance, and Process Goals

on improving the agents' knowledge of the various products, and they would build the agents' confidence.

The team beat their previous year's figures by 21 percent, and not only did the team win the award by a large margin, they also enhanced the skills, knowledge, and confidence required to sustain high performance going forward.

Figure 13.2, on the following page, provides an example of how this approach helped a senior manager I coached, Eric, plan his career development. The process involved identifying his outcome goal, followed by the performance goals that would give him the best chance of achieving the outcome goal. Eric and I then worked on process goals that would enable him to achieve the performance goals; these would also form his day-to-day focus.

The outcome goal Eric set was to achieve a senior leadership position in his current company within three years. This was not under his control because he would be competing with colleagues who had similar aspirations.

The performance goals Eric generated covered a number of areas: being visionary, an influencer, decisive, a team builder, credible, having presence, being confident, and achieving a

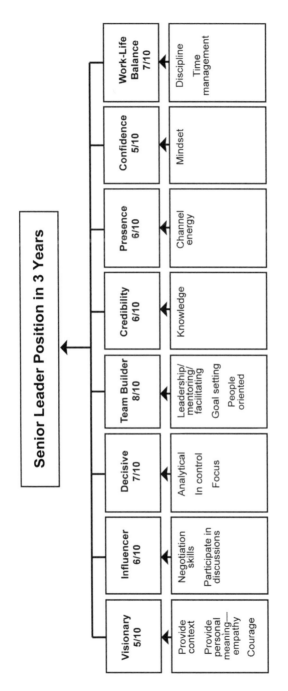

Figure 13.2 Eric's Path to Becoming a Senior Leader

good work-life balance. These would ensure he hit the criteria he figured would put him in the best possible position to achieve his outcome goal. These were the goals under his control. We then worked through a simple scoring process in which he rated himself from 1 to 10 on each performance goal. These ratings represented his current ability in each area.

The process goals underpinned the delivery of each performance goal:

- **Being visionary.** Eric's 5 out of 10 rating reflected his awareness that this was an area that needed significant focus. He set process goals around being able to identify a compelling vision for his people that would provide context for the future and generate personal meaning in terms of how they could contribute to achieving it. He also recognized that an important part of this process would be building what he called "courage" to take on this visibility and accountability.

- **Being an influencer.** This was a 6 out of 10 for Eric, and he targeted internal business development meetings as the starting point for participating more in debates and making his voice heard. He had a specific process goal of enhancing his negotiation skills to help structure his input.

- **Being decisive.** Eric thought he was pretty decisive, rating it a 7 out of 10, but still wanted to work on it further. He felt he needed to hone his powers of analysis of situations, stay in control of his thoughts when making decisions under pressure, and stay focused and not get distracted from making them.

- **Being an effective team builder.** Eric thought this was one of his strengths, scoring it 8 out of 10. He wanted to further enhance his competence in this area by focusing more on his people's needs, helping them set effective goals, and practicing being a leader, mentor, and facilitator when opportunities arose.

- **Having credibility.** Eric scored himself a 6 out of 10, recognizing that he needed to improve his knowledge of other areas of the business to gain what he perceived to be credibility among his colleagues.

- **Having presence.** This was another 6 out of 10 for Eric, who wanted to have a greater presence and make more of an impact around the office. For him, there was a need to channel his energy and enthusiasm toward meeting the needs of his people.

- **Being confident.** Eric's confidence waned from time to time, which is why he only rated himself at 5. His process goal was to develop a more positive mindset, beginning with building his self-esteem.

- **Achieving a good work-life balance.** Eric thought he had quite a good work-life balance, scoring it a 7, but he recognized he would need to be even more disciplined and manage his time even better if he was to be an effective leader in the future.

The process goals provided his day-to-day focus, and we built in a measurement and regular review process that enabled him to monitor his progress toward his performance goals on a regular basis. Eric achieved a senior leadership role in just over two years.

Starting with the end in mind is fundamental to the process of setting effective goals. This top-down approach involves identifying the desired outcome, associated performances, and then the key underlying processes that will enable their achievement. However, putting the plan into action on a day-to-day basis requires a bottom-up approach, with your major focus being on processes.

The continual focus on getting the processes right will eventually deliver the performances and outcomes.

So What Will You Do?

Channeling your motivation so it works *for* rather than *against* you is best achieved by ensuring your goals are INSPIRED, and also by setting outcome goals and planning how they will be achieved via aligned performance and process goals. Time-Out 13 provides the opportunity for you to apply these frameworks to help you plan your development as a *real* leader.

TIME-OUT 13

DEVELOPING AS A *REAL* LEADER

- What is your outcome goal in your role as a *real* leader? When do you want to achieve it?

- What performance goals will ensure progress toward your outcome goal? Make sure they are things you can totally control.

- What process goals will underpin the delivery of each performance goal? These process goals should provide a day-to-day focus.

- How will you measure and review your progress?

- Ensure that your goals are INSPIRED goals: I(nternalized), N(urturing), S(pecific), P(lanned), I(n your control), R(eviewed regularly), E(nergizing), D(ocumented).

Setting goals is a powerful tool to help you thrive on pressure. You will always be clear about what you want to achieve and how. When used effectively, goal-setting will drive you toward achieving your long-term aspirations, as well as providing you with a day-to-day focus that ensures you make continual progress toward them.

KEY TAKEAWAYS

- Goal setting, when used effectively, is a powerful tool for channeling motivation.
- Goals provide the drive and discipline for *real* leaders to persevere in the face of adversity and to bounce back after failure.
- INSPIRED goals will deliver sustained high motivation and performance.
- Starting with the end in mind is the most effective approach to setting outcome, performance, and process goals.
- Process goals drive your day-to-day focus.

That Concludes Master Class 4

That is the conclusion of Master Class 4. You have explored what drives your motivation and learned about the importance of maximizing your internal drivers. You have also been provided with strong evidence for the need to set goals that channel your motivation. Remember, it is not your *level* of motivation that lies at the core of being a *real* leader, but rather the *nature* of your motivation.

Master Class 5

■ ■ ■

Directing Your Focus to the Things That *Really* Matter in Your Role as a *Real* Leader

OBJECTIVES

■ To help you identify where your focus is and what you should be focused on as a *real* leader

■ To equip you with strategies and tools to help you maintain your focus on the things that *really* matter in your role as a *real* leader

■ To provide you with tools to enable you to switch your focus on and off

■ ■ ■

Chapter 14

■ ■ ■

What *Should* You Be Focused On?

KEY TOPICS

■ The distractions that threaten your focus as a *real* leader
■ What focus is
■ What *real* leaders focus on

Babe Ruth was in a batting slump, and his team looked like they were about to be knocked out of the World Series. He was two strikes down, and the pressure on him was made worse by a very loud spectator behind the batting plate who was giving him a hard time. Ruth hit the next pitch out of the park.

Ruth was quizzed by reporters after the game on what he was thinking about as he stood at the plate with only one chance left. Was he thinking about the pressure on him because he was on the verge of being struck out? Was he thinking about how much his team was depending on him to get them out of the crisis they were in? Was he thinking about the guy in the crowd who was giving him abuse? Ruth assured them that none of these things entered his head. He was focused on hitting the ball!

The takeaway message from this story about Babe Ruth is that there was plenty going on that could have distracted him as the pitcher was winding up to release the ball. Fortunately, Ruth was able to focus on what he *should* have been focused on and on what *really* mattered—hitting the ball.

As a *real* leader, there will be many things vying for your attention. In fact, there are so many things that leaders often fall into the trap of not knowing what they *should* be focusing on, and there is a danger that extraneous, irrelevant, and relatively unimportant factors can intrude on their effectiveness.

A number of years ago I coached Jim, the leader of a company in the pharmaceutical industry. He had taken over a struggling business five years earlier and had led it to double-digit growth in each of the past three years. Here was a thriving operation headed by a *real* leader who had put his neck on the line. The company's success was rudely interrupted when news broke one day about serious problems with one of its new drugs. The hype in the media increased rapidly as more and more people came forward to tell their stories of problems with the drug. My coaching conversations with Jim centered largely around what the media were saying and the impact it might have on the business. My role was to challenge him on where his focus was, and where it should be. We identified factors outside his control, one of which was the media; he quickly realized he was wasting valuable time and energy focusing on something he could do nothing about. What he *could* control was what was happening within the business; he focused on his people's morale and what he could do to reassure them during this difficult period. Now he was being a *real* leader and focusing on the things that *really* mattered.

The best *real* leaders focus on the things that *really* matter rather than what shouts loudest for their attention. It is difficult to thrive on pressure when you cannot see the forest for the trees! This chapter will help you to recognize what you *currently* focus on compared to what you *should* be focused on.

A Few Things You Should Know About Focus

This section covers a few things you should know about focus before moving on to what you *should* be focusing on.

What Is Focus?

The word *focus* is used freely and frequently; most people have a vague sense of what it is, but few are able to define it. In its simplest definition, *focus* describes the clear, vivid thoughts and images that occupy your conscious mind at any one moment. Switching focus involves withdrawing thoughts and images from some things and directing them to deal effectively with others.

You Only Have So Much of It

Focus presents a challenge to all leaders because there is simply not enough of it to deal with all of the things demanding their attention. Focus has a limited capacity that is actually quite small and exists in your conscious mind. For example, while reading this paragraph, it is very difficult for you to think about anything else, and if you are thinking about something else, then you are not focused on the content of this paragraph. In other words, you can only hold and think about a small amount of information at any one time. So where you direct your focus is pretty important.

Focusing on Pressure

You already know that as a *real* leader there are so many different things fighting for your attention that it is sometimes very difficult to keep it directed toward what *really* matters. And it is even harder to remain focused on the things that *really* matter when the pressure is intense. Pressure, in itself, can be a major threat to your focus. The exposure that comes with being a *real* leader, for example, might be enough to distract you. It is an especially dangerous threat to *safe* leaders whose focus on the potential consequences of failure, or how they *must* be successful, distracts them from focusing on what really matters in delivering the *real* leadership required.

The Effects of Past and Future Focus

Your focus is sometimes dominated by things that occurred in the past that you just cannot let go of. Alex was a leader in a telecommunications company that had just undergone a structural reorganization. The change resulted in one of Alex's peers being promoted so that he was now Alex's boss. Alex liked his new boss and had always worked well with him as a peer. But Alex believed he was more capable than his new leader and was angry about being overlooked for the position. Our coaching sessions became dominated by Alex's failure to accept the situation. It was clear that his focus was not on his day-to-day performance, but on the circumstances surrounding the earlier restructure. Alex's anger impacted negatively on his relationship with his boss, and it became an obstacle to his own effectiveness.

For another leader I coached, it was not the past that distracted her; it was the future. Jessica was the global head of a professional services firm and had just heard on the grapevine that the organization was being targeted as a potential acquisition. It was only speculation, but Jessica spent virtually all her time focusing on this possible takeover and the implications for herself and the organization. Jessica's mind was not on her day-to-day responsibilities, and her direct reports became frustrated by her lack of responsiveness to their operational needs. She was being distracted by the future, and it was impacting negatively on her leadership.

These are classic cases of leaders who were focusing on the wrong things; worse still, it was having a debilitating effect on their leadership and performance. The examples of Alex and Jessica demonstrate how it is very easy to be distracted from delivering your best as a leader. They also emphasize that it is not just factors in the current environment that compete for your attention; past and future events, and how you think about them, can also dominate your focus and impair your effectiveness as a leader—if you let them!

You *Should* Be Focusing on Creating a High-Performance Environment

I described in Chapter 3 how *real* leaders recognize they are no longer being employed to be a good engineer, or accountant, or lawyer. They realize they are now in a position where their mission is to lead people. Their responsibility lies in creating environments where high performance is inevitable and sustainable. *Real* leaders focus on the way they lead, on providing their people with the tools to do the job, and on inspiring them to want to do a good job.

If you are to become the *real* leader you aspire to, then your focus *should* be on the following:

- Providing vision, challenge, *and* support to your people

- Getting the strategic focus right

- Ensuring your people have the appropriate talents and skills to enable them to contribute to delivering your vision

- Providing your people with the appropriate tools to enable them to do their jobs effectively

- Inspiring your people so they are engaged with and committed to your vision and the organization

- Minimizing the constraints on your people so they can thrive

- Maximizing your people's supports

These are the things that should drive your focus; they constitute the key performance indicators against which you should be measured.

Some Guiding Principles for Your Day-to-Day Focus as a *Real* Leader

Enhancing your ability to achieve an "appropriate" day-to-day focus in your role as a *real* leader involves directing your attention toward what you *should* be thinking about to be effective. I am sure this will seem very obvious and merely common sense. The problem however is that common sense is not always common practice, especially where focus is concerned. You will know, for example, that it is not helpful during those final moments before an important presentation, negotiation, or interview to think about the mistakes you might make and other things that might go wrong. Instead, you *should* be focusing on things like how well prepared you are, the opportunity (as opposed to threat) that lies ahead, and the skills and abilities that make you good at what you do. However, people like myself are in demand because some leaders struggle to understand what they *should* be focused on and then how to control their focus.

An "appropriate" focus can vary enormously from situation to situation, from leader to leader, and from second to second depending on the specific circumstances you face. Generalizing is difficult, therefore, but the best *real* leaders I have coached can be characterized as having a number of guiding principles that help to direct their focus. Try applying them to your own set of circumstances.

- **Focus on what you can control.** "Controlling the controllables" is a phrase used frequently to emphasize that devoting any of that valuable, limited-capacity focus to things you just cannot control is a waste of your time and energy. Accept that there are things in the environment you cannot influence, identify what they are, and then focus on the things you *can* control.

- **Focus on processes.** Focus on getting the processes right. In particular, focus on the process of leading by example and providing a good role model for your people.

- **Focus on the present.** Focusing on the past, whether it be mistakes or setbacks, makes no sense. They are history. You can do nothing to change them, so why beat yourself up about them? Accept they have happened, "bin" them, and move on.

- **Focus on strengths.** As a *real* leader, potential external distractions exist in abundance, but there are also internal ones that lurk menacingly in the background. Doubts about your ability to deliver under pressure is an example of something that will drag your focus away from what you *should* be focused on. Focus on your strengths and let them come to the fore.

- **Focus on positives.** You will be surrounded by people with a range of personalities and mindsets. Some of them will have a negative influence on you and the environment you lead in. Do not let them drag you into their world of skepticism and negativity. Identify the positives in the environment surrounding you and focus on them.

- **Focus on staying calm.** A simple focus on remaining calm and composed when the pressures of being a *real* leader are becoming excessive can be a very effective tool. I described in Chapter 6 how a quick relaxation tool based on focusing on a mantra or key word (such as "relax" or "calm") as you breathe out is very helpful in achieving a composed state. Think about using that tool as a way to help you control your focus when you feel the pressure mounting.

So What Will You Do?

The guiding principles described above will serve as useful reminders of the things you *should* be focusing on when the pressure is on. Spend a few minutes working through Time-Out 14 to identify how you will put them into practice.

TIME-OUT 14

WHAT *SHOULD* YOU BE FOCUSED ON?

- **Identify the things in your work environment that are potential distractions from your focus on being a *real* leader.**

---

continued

- What things from your past, or perhaps the future, distract you?

- Of all the things that demand your attention in your day-to-day role as a *real* leader, what are the things that *really* matter and deserve your focus?

- Which of the guiding principles will you put into practice?

This chapter has highlighted how focus is a limited resource, so how you direct your focus is very important. The following chapter describes strategies and tools for controlling your focus.

KEY TAKEAWAYS

- In its simplest definition, *focus* describes the clear, vivid thoughts and images that occupy your conscious mind at any one moment.
- Switching focus involves withdrawing thoughts and images from some things and directing them to deal effectively with others.
- Some leaders waste time and energy focusing on things that are irrelevant to what they are trying to achieve.
- *Real* leaders focus on what they can control, processes, the present, strengths, positives, and staying calm under intense pressure.

Chapter 15

■ ■ ■

Controlling Your Focus

KEY TOPICS

■ Unhelpful and helpful focus as a *real* leader
■ Achieving optimal focus
■ Tools and strategies for maintaining and regaining focus

Focus is a limited-capacity resource that you must use very carefully. It should be clear by now that it is not sufficient to know *what* you should be focused on as a *real* leader—you also need to be able to *control* your focus. *Real* leaders who are mentally tough have high levels of control over their focus and where they direct it. They are able to maintain, and regain when necessary, an appropriate focus at times when there are numerous potential distractions. There are several aspects of focus that are key to developing and enhancing your mental toughness so you can perform your *real* leadership role effectively. These, together with related strategies and tools for maintaining and regaining focus, are described in this chapter.

Dealing with the Distractions That Are Part of Being a *Real* Leader

Your day-to-day functioning will be full of predictable distractions that go with the territory of being a *real* leader. These will be specific to your role and circumstances but are likely to include things like those continual interruptions by colleagues appearing at your desk, receiving a hoard of e-mails and voice-mails that all require your immediate attention, being pounced on as you make your way to the coffee machine by direct reports who need your advice, and those requests for your attendance at meetings that you know you do not need to be at.

The important thing about managing these distractions is to expect rather than be surprised by them, and to have a plan for how to deal with them. Simple strategies and tools you can use are:

- **Accept the existence of distractions.** Distractions are part of being a *real* leader, so accept they exist. There is little point in trying to ignore them because this effort alone will take up some of your valuable focus.

- **Set time aside to deal with distractions.** Build time into your schedule to deal exclusively with those things that are important and maybe urgent to your people, but which do not have the same level of importance or urgency for yourself. Let your people know when these times are, and then adhere to them.

- **Remind yourself about what *really* matters.** Recognize distractions and when you are focusing on them. Past mistakes, setbacks, and things you cannot control are just a few examples of unhelpful distractions. Identify what *really* matters in your quest to build a high-performance environment where your people can thrive.

- **Ask yourself if you are focusing on what *really* matters.** Asking yourself the simple question, "Am I focusing on what *really* matters?" acts as an effective trigger to refocus, if necessary, on the things you *should* be focusing on. Some leaders I work with use small self-adhesive colored dots (readily available from stationery sections of supermarkets) as a visual stimulus to pose this question to themselves. Typically, they have stuck them on equipment and accessories they use frequently during the working day, such as cell phones or computer screens.

Staying on Track in the Face of Potential Derailers

Unfortunately, not all distractions are predictable. They can be unexpected and uncontrollable, appearing from nowhere so that you are completely derailed by them. I have witnessed leaders who become derailed by events such as the unexpected news of the takeover of the company, or discovering that their slide presentation has been wiped from their laptop computer minutes before a pitch for a big piece of business. Worse still was the discovery by one leader that a direct report had just made a mistake that would cost the organization a lot of money.

When unexpected and uncontrollable events or circumstances occur, it is important to regain your composure as quickly as possible and continue with minimal disruption toward your desired goal. This is where leaders like you can learn a lot from elite athletes who have developed effective tools and strategies for such situations. Two that are particularly effective are:

- **"What ifs."** This tool involves identifying those things that could go wrong in important situations. Work out what you would do in these tricky circumstances before you encounter them. These plans will take the decision making away from the heat of the situation when the pressure may cause you to act rashly.

- **Mental rehearsal.** "What ifs" are even more effective tools for dealing with unexpected, uncontrollable events if you mentally rehearse what you will do beforehand. Why not try this by identifying the things that could go wrong in a client pitch and what you would do in each instance. Then form a mental image of each so you have a carefully rehearsed strategy for regaining your focus for anything that might go wrong.

The tools described above may sound a little strange in the world of business where such things may appear a bit "touchy-feely." Give them a chance and experiment with them. You may be surprised at how effective they can be in helping you remain composed and focused in the most pressured situations.

Compartmentalizing *Real* Leadership and Setting Time Aside to Deal with the Other Things Going on in Your Life

Real leadership does not occur in a vacuum. You have another life outside work that should be even more important. And there will be times when your different worlds overlap and sometimes collide. Being mentally tough means you are able to prevent events and circumstances outside work from distracting you when you are performing your *real* leader role. Relationships, births, deaths, financial affairs, and whatever else may be happening are all important elements of life that cannot be ignored. But there are times to focus on them and times to switch off from them! Compartmentalizing the different aspects of your life is important if you are going to deliver *real* leadership that is sustainable. The tools and strategies described below will help you in developing and enhancing your ability to achieve this:

- **Setting time aside to deal with the other things in your life.** Devote the necessary time to deal with personal life issues, or they will linger and be a constant source of distraction. Make sure it is quality time that will enable you to tackle the issues head-on.

- **Pressing the focus switch to "on."** This simple tool involves imagining a switch, similar to a light switch, which actually turns your *real* leadership focus on. Imagine pressing the switch to the "on" position to focus you on the things that *really* matter. Believe it or not, a few leaders I have coached have actually carried a small light switch around with them in their pockets to help them, quite literally, switch on their focus and direct it to their *real* leadership duties and accountabilities when required.

The key to using these tools effectively lies in ensuring you park thoughts about what is happening outside your leadership arena and then have the discipline to return to deal with them. If not, they will merely become convenient avoidance strategies that result in issues never being addressed head-on.

Recharging Your Focus on Being a *Real* Leader

Leaders who are mentally tough know about the importance of not only switching their *real* leadership focus on, but also switching it off. This could be at the end of each day, or it may be in the form of taking regular vacations where the BlackBerry is left at home. This reduces the risk of burnout and also helps to instill a more balanced perspective on work and life. Work-life balance, and making time for the other things and people that matter outside your work environment, has been a common topic when I have coached *real* leaders. Sadly, many do not achieve the successful balance they are striving so desperately for, and this can have serious consequences for their home life and sometimes their performance at work. The approaches described below will be useful in helping you to switch off from the pressure of delivering sustained *real* leadership, and also enable you to achieve a healthy work-life balance:

- **Planning restoration time.** Restoration is crucial if you are to deliver *real* leadership that is sustainable. In the same way that your body needs rest so it can recharge itself, so, too, does your mind. Relentless pressure will take its toll in the form of mental fatigue and reduced power of concentration. It becomes increasingly difficult to focus over sustained periods, and the only answer is a time-out. Relaxing vacations are one obvious means of restoring the mind's energy in readiness for a renewed focus. Planning regular vacations in your calendar therefore is an important way of recharging your focus. Another way is to plan times in your weekly schedule where you will switch off from work.

- **Pressing the focus switch to "off."** I described earlier how using a switch, either physically or metaphorically, is a useful tool for switching your *real* leadership focus on. The switch can also be used to turn your focus on being a *real* leader off. This will prove particularly helpful in the early stages of working toward a better work-life balance.

These tools and strategies are no more than common sense, but it is easy to forget about your need for them. When you are under pressure for long periods you are probably unable to find the time for them anyway! This is when you will most need these time-outs, so plan them into your calendar.

Getting Back on Track Following Failures and Successes

Failures are an obvious threat to a any leader's focus. The despondency and blaming that can follow failures is paralyzing and an obstacle to focusing on what *really* matters. Successes also bring with them the risk of being a distraction to future focus because they can lead to complacency and spending too much time celebrating them. *Real* leaders who are mentally tough make sure they allocate time to deal with both failures and successes.

Learning from Failure

Real leaders seldom beat themselves up after failures, but they *are* careful to identify and analyze the causes. This process involves drawing out the learning points before leaving the failure behind as history and moving on armed with their learning.

The key messages for *you* in dealing with failures are:

- Do not beat yourself up!

- Identify and analyze the causes.

- Draw out the learning points to take forward.

- Leave the failure behind as history.

These processes will ensure you deal fully and effectively with failures so you do not carry any unwanted disappointment or despondency into the future.

Celebrating Success and Then Moving On

Mentally tough *real* leaders make time to celebrate their successes. Some leaders and their teams I have worked with have put as much effort into their celebrations as they did into their achievements! And why not? They work hard to deliver the highest levels of performance and need to take time out to reflect on what they have accomplished. These leaders are also aware that devoting too much time to their celebrations can cause a complacency that distracts them and their people. They know when to stop celebrating and move on to the next challenge.

Before moving on, however, these leaders are careful to scrutinize and understand thoroughly the reasons underpinning their success. In this way, they are able to build further on their strengths and recognize and continually replicate those things that underpin their achievements.

The key messages for *you* in dealing with successes are:

- Spend time celebrating them!

- Scrutinize and understand the reasons for your successes.

- Use these to build on your strengths so that you will reproduce them in the future.

- Know when to stop celebrating and move on to the next challenge.

These processes will ensure you deal effectively with successes so that you celebrate them appropriately but do not take any complacency into the future.

So What Will You Do?

This chapter has described a number of strategies and tools that will help you to control that vital limited-capacity resource that is your focus. Devote a good chunk of time to working through Time-Out 15 and figure out some specific actions you will take forward.

TIME-OUT 15

CONTROLLING YOUR FOCUS

This chapter has covered the following tools and strategies for controlling your focus:

- Dealing with the predictable distractions that are part of being a *real* leader

- Recovering from unexpected, uncontrollable events

- Compartmentalizing your *real* leader role and setting time aside to deal with the other things going on in your life

- Recharging your focus

- Dealing with failures and successes

Which of these strategies and tools, or elements of different ones, most appeal to you? In what situations and circumstances will it or they be most useful? How do you intend to put it or them into practice?

Remember that you only have so much focus, so stay in control of it and use it very carefully.

KEY TAKEAWAYS

- It is not sufficient to know what you *should be* focused on as a *real* leader—you also need to be able to *control* your focus.
- *Real* leaders who are mentally tough have high levels of control over their focus.
- There are a number of aspects of focus that are key to enhancing your mental toughness as a *real* leader:
  - Dealing with the predictable distractions that are part of being a *real* leader
  - Recovering from unexpected, uncontrollable events
  - Compartmentalizing your *real* leader role and setting time aside to deal with the other things going on in your life
  - Recharging your focus
  - Dealing with failures and successes

That Concludes Master Class 5

This is the conclusion of Master Class 5. You are in the position of knowing what you *should* be focusing on as a *real* leader. Your challenge is to stay focused on those things and not get distracted by the multitude of other things that will fight for your attention. The strategies and tools for controlling your focus will be of enormous help in maintaining and regaining your focus when required. Be sure to put them into practice.

Over to You

■ ■ ■

Your
Real Leader
Toolkit

Chapter 16

■ ■ ■

Your *Real* Leader Toolkit

KEY TOPICS

■ A reminder about the choices you are committing
to as a *real* leader

■ The core principles you should follow in creating
a high-performance environment

■ The tools you can use to help you thrive on
pressure

The five master classes have covered a substantial amount of
ground. This concluding chapter draws together their content in
the form of a toolkit of reminders about the choices you are committing to as a *real* leader, the core principles you should follow in
creating a high-performance environment, and the tools you can
use to develop and enhance your ability to thrive on pressure.

The Choices You Have Made to Be a *Real* Leader

Being a *real* leader is not easy, which is why too many incum-
bents of leadership positions, knowingly or unknowingly, go
for the easier option of *safe* leadership. By reading this book
you have opted to be a *real* leader and in doing so have made a
number of choices you will need to remind yourself of from time
to time.

- **Your Choice to Take on the Pressure**

Your choice to take on the visibility of *real* leadership means you will be exposed to sometimes relentless pressure that can cause you to feel isolated, lonely, and vulnerable. And that is just during normal times! During economic downturns and when market conditions are tough, you will be stretched to the limits of your capability and resourcefulness. At times like these, it may be hard to see beyond the pressures your responsibilities bring with them. You will need to remind yourself why you have chosen this path: the internal drivers that provide positive challenge, the change you bring about because you have the guts to do it, the development you see in your people because you give them the opportunities, and the individual care you provide that makes your people feel valued.

- **Your Choice to Be Accountable When Things Go Wrong**

By being a *real* leader, the buck stops with you! Your people's failures are *your* failures—you are the one who is accountable. Have the courage to seek to understand the causes of failure so that you can learn from them and take your learning forward.

- **Your Choice to Accept That You Will Make Mistakes**

You have chosen to put yourself in a position where you are expected to innovate and take calculated risks. You will sometimes get it wrong and you will make mistakes. These are what will make you a better and stronger *real* leader, as long as you see mistakes as a key part of your learning and development.

- **Your Choice to Do What Is Right**

  You are aware of your responsibility to make those difficult, often critical, decisions that might not be popular with everyone, but are the right thing to do. You know that no matter how hard you try, there will always be someone who is unhappy with your leadership. There may even be people who think they can do the job better than you. No matter what, it is important that you tackle hard issues head-on.

- **Your Choice to Drive Change**

  No individual, team, or organization can ever stand still. Sustained success is underpinned by constant change that takes you to the next level. As a *real* leader, your responsibility is to lead by example in driving continuous change. Encourage challenge and collective problem-solving among your people because you cannot do it all on your own.

- **Your Choice to Be a Role Model**

  Role modeling is a critical part of your role as a *real* leader. Role model what you want to see and hear in your people, and also role model the aspirations of the organization. If you want your people to raise their performance bars, then raise your own. Show them you are hungry for feedback because it is so important to your development. And recognize and celebrate success in a way that inspires them to want more.

- **Your Choice to Develop the People You Lead So That They May Someday Be Your Boss**

  If you do a great job of being a *real* leader you may find that one day you are being led by someone who used to follow *you*. Your choice to empower and coach your people, combined with encouraging them to be creative and innovative, will enable them to make a significant contribution to achieving your vision. It will also help their individual development as they pursue their own aspirations in the organization. The best of them may end up being your leader! Take huge satisfaction from this.

Your Role in Creating a High-Performance Environment

Real leaders create environments where high performance is inevitable and sustainable. If you are to achieve this goal, there are a number of core principles you should remember and follow.

- **Accept That You Can No Longer Do All the Things That Got You to Where You Are**

  This is where some leaders get it wrong. Most are promoted to leadership positions because they are functional experts, and they make the mistake of continuing to be involved in the detail because they enjoy and are good at it. But, as you know, leadership is about people, and not about managing a function. As a *real* leader, your role is to create the conditions for your people to thrive. Minimizing constraints and maximizing supports for your people is a critical role that will help them deliver the performance you are now leading and no longer doing yourself.

- **Identify and Communicate a Compelling Vision**

  Your people want to know where you intend to take them. Figure out what your vision is and communicate it in a way that makes sense, and also demonstrates a passion that will inspire your people to follow you and find a way of delivering it even in the most trying circumstances.

- **Get the Strategic Focus Right**

  You will have to manage the dynamic tension of current versus future focus. Your responsibility is to focus on the longer term; specifically, the innovation and well-being the future health of the organization is dependent on. Of course, your focus will be dragged into the current, day-to-day detail, especially when times are tough, but do not fall into the trap of getting stuck there.

- **Make Sure You Have the Right People in the Right Roles**

  If you are to stay out of the detail, you need to have people with the appropriate knowledge, skills, and experience in the appropriate roles. This is your responsibility, and achieving this will provide you with the space you require to focus on your job as a *real* leader.

- **Clearly Define and Communicate What Is Expected of Them**

  Having the right people in the right roles is insufficient—they must know what you expect from them. They want to know what their short-term focus should be and how their individual performances will contribute to achieving the longer-term aspirations and vision of the organization.

- **Have the Courage to Let Go**

  If you have the right people in the right roles, and they know what is expected of them, have the courage to place your confidence and trust in them to deliver the goods. This will probably feel strange at first as you struggle with relinquishing some control. And it will not be possible before you have the confidence and trust in yourself to pass it on to your people.

- **Balance Vision, Challenge, and Support**

  Once you have everything in place, your day-to-day role as a *real* leader is to remind people of the vision, challenge them to deliver against it, and support them in doing so. Remember that if you can get the balance right, you will create an environment where people's potential is unleashed and high performance is inevitable and sustainable.

- **Be Mentally Tough**

  As you already know, the pressure inextricably linked to the principles above means you need to have a robust and resilient mental toughness that will help you thrive in these conditions.

Thrive on Pressure

Remember that pressure brings out the best and the worst in all of us. You have chosen to be a *real* leader, and now you have another choice about how you will let the inevitable and inescapable pressure affect you. You have reached the point where you know a lot about how mental toughness is the key to thriving on pressure and being a great *real* leader. As you strive to use your mental toughness to help you thrive on the pressure of being a *real* leader, remember that you now have a vast array of tools at your disposal. Here is a reminder of them.

Stay in Control Under Stress

Unfortunately, there will be times when the pressure that comes with being a *real* leader is so relentless and overwhelming that stress is an inevitable consequence. Remember there are three ways you can deal with your stress:

1. **Keep your stress symptoms under control.**

    Tools you have learned about are:

    - Monitoring your stress so you know when to cope

    - Using meditative relaxation to calm your troubled mind

    - Using mental imagery to help you to relax

    - Using abdominal breathing to control any tension

    - Recognizing how your behavior changes when you are stressed and adapting it accordingly

    - Working on achieving a healthy lifestyle

2. **Challenge the thinking that causes you stress.**

    Tools you have learned about are:

- Using thought-stopping statements to block out automatic negative thoughts

- Reframing your stinking thinking using trigger questions, reminding yourself that you have a choice about the way you think, and imagining what you would say to a close friend who was experiencing the same thoughts

- Asking for support from trusted and respected people in your life who can help you view things from a different perspective

3. **Tackle the sources of your stress.**

   Tools you have learned about are:

   - Making things happen in the form of tackling issues head-on, which involves challenging your assumptions and making tough decisions

   - Creating choices that change situations rather than fulfilling obligations that cause you stress

   - Focusing on minimizing the constraints in your control, as well as maximizing your supports

Strengthen Your Self-Belief

Thriving on pressure is easier if you believe in yourself. Believe in your ability as a *real* leader so you can be open to challenges and new ideas, make those difficult and sometimes unpopular decisions, challenge orthodoxy, and make yourself even more visible during tough times. Remember that you have tools at your disposal to help you build your self-esteem and boost your self-confidence.

1. **Build your self-esteem.**

   Tools you have learned about are:

   - Viewing feedback as developmental and about your behavior, rather than negative and about you as a person

   - Taking appropriate personal credit for your successes rather than attributing them to luck or some external factor

   - Recalling and celebrating your achievements, both as a person and as a leader

   - Trying not to be perfect

2. **Boost your self-confidence.**

   Tools you have learned about are:

   - Focusing on your recent successes over the past few days, weeks, or perhaps months

   - Ensuring quick wins through setting short-term goals

   - Drawing on your experiences of being successful in situations similar to those you encounter

   - Mentally rehearsing how you will deal with pressure situations before you experience them

- Learning from other people's successes and how they deal with pressure situations

- Changing negative self-talk by using positive counter-statements

- Interpreting intense mental and physical responses to pressure as helping you to prepare

Channel Your Motivation to Work for You

It is not your *level* of motivation that is important but rather the *nature* of it. High motivation that is "unhealthy," in the form of desperation or fear, can actually work against you. Your motivation needs to be "healthy" for you to be able to thrive on pressure. This is also what enables you to bounce back from setbacks and disappointments. The tools you have learned that will ensure your motivation works *for* rather than *against* you are:

- Exploring the foundations of your motivation in terms of approach versus avoidance, internal versus external, and whether you enjoy your quest for success versus being desperate to succeed

- Maximizing your internal motivation by satisfying your needs for feeling competent, having autonomy, and feeling a sense of belonging to your organization, business unit, and/or team

- Setting goals that are INSPIRED (Internalized, Nurturing, Specific, Planned, In your control, Reviewed regularly, Energizing, and Documented)

- Setting outcome, performance, and process goals that are completely aligned and which provide a long-, mid- and short-term focus

Direct Your Focus to the Things That Really Matter

As a *real* leader, there are so many things competing for your attention that it is sometimes difficult to remain focused on what you should be focused on. You only have so much focus, so make sure you direct it to the things that *really* matter. The tools you have learned to help you control your focus are:

- Figuring out what you *should* be focused on so that you are able to recognize when you are being distracted

- Focusing on creating a high-performance environment because this is what *real* leaders do

- Having a day-to-day focus on processes, positives, what you can control, and staying calm under pressure

- Devoting time to deal with those inevitable distractions that are part of being a *real* leader

- Staying on track in the face of potential derailers in the form of unexpected and uncontrollable distractions

- Compartmentalizing your *real* leader role and setting time aside to deal with the other things going on in your life

- Recharging your focus by planning restoration time and pressing the focus switch to "off"

- Getting back on track following failures and successes

Over to You

Being able to thrive on pressure will mean that being a *real* leader will be stimulating, energizing, and, perhaps most important, enjoyable. And when you get it right, being a *real* leader will also provide you with an enormous sense of satisfaction and achievement. It really is something worth striving for. Good luck!

KEY TAKEAWAY

Apply your enhanced mental toughness to be an even better *real* leader.

Index

■ ■ ■

About the Author

■ ■ ■

Professor Graham Jones's experience of consulting with high-level performers spans more than twenty years. It includes working closely with Olympic and world champions from a variety of sports, military personnel, and senior leaders and their teams in Fortune 500 and FTSE 100 companies.

Graham has more than 150 publications in the area of high-level performance. Among these are four books, numerous groundbreaking studies in scientific journals, and articles that demystify and unravel complex concepts and theories in human performance psychology, making them easy to apply in the workplace. His article "How the Best of the Best Get Better and Better," published in *Harvard Business Review*, received wide acclaim for capturing the essence of sustained high performance that all business leaders aspire to.

Since cofounding Lane4 Management Group, a leading performance development consultancy, in 1995, Graham has been very active as a coach of high-profile leaders and their teams. He works on large-scale initiatives around organizational change, mergers and acquisitions, and global rollouts of people-development programs.

Visit www.sustainedhighperformance.com for updates and news.